The Right to Movement

The Right to Movement
Motor Development in Every School

David Stewart

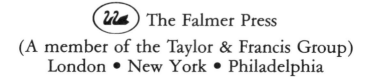 The Falmer Press
(A member of the Taylor & Francis Group)
London • New York • Philadelphia

UK The Falmer Press, Rankine Road, Basingstoke, Hants RG24 0PR

USA The Falmer Press, Taylor & Francis Inc., 242 Cherry Street,
Philadelphia, PA 19106-1906

First published 1990

British Library Cataloguing in Publication Data

Stewart, David
  The right to movement.
  1. Children. Motor skills. Development.
  Physiological aspects.
  I. Title
  612.76

  ISBN 1–85000–526–5
  ISBN 1–85000–527–3 pbk

Typeset in 12/14 Garamond by
Chapterhouse, The Cloisters, Formby L37 3PX
Printed and bound in Great Britain by
Redwood Press Limited, Melksham, Wiltshire

Contents

Introduction

Withdrawing children from one lesson to enable them to receive instruction or assistance in another subject somewhere else is not an unusual feature of school life. Occasionally however, the slight inconvenience of this can set one thinking. For example, in September 1985, I began teaching physical education in a '6 to 16' special school for children with moderate learning difficulties. The first real sign that this new job was not to be entirely straightforward came when I was asked to release one child from her physical education lesson so that she might be seen by the physiotherapist.

My first thought was that the child was suffering from a sports injury but, 'surely not,' I said to myself, 'she's only eight years old!' I was told, 'she needs to be released each week, I'm afraid. She has a regular appointment with the physiotherapist'.

'Oh yes, why's that?'
'Because she's a clumsy child'.

I was intrigued. What exactly did that phrase 'clumsy child' mean? What makes a child 'clumsy'? How is 'clumsy' defined? What are the effects of 'clumsiness', both upon the child and other people? How many 'clumsy' children are there? Are they numerous in non-special schools? All these and a dozen more questions occurred to me almost at once, and I thought it was worthy of further investigation. My starting point was the immediate situation and I approached the physiotherapist to find out. Why was a pupil being removed from physical education, I asked, to be given her own personal physical education lesson? Again the answer came back — 'she's a clumsy child'. The physiotherapist then reeled off the names of another seven children she would be seeing that day, adding that, in her view, this was only the 'tip of the iceberg'. She explained further that the children who were being treated in our school had been referred to her by their general practitioner as 'potentially clumsy' children. I found the phrase 'potentially clumsy' vague. It told me little or nothing concrete about the children involved, and so it was at this point I decided that there was a need for a greater understanding of what was going on.

Now I'm afraid that I somewhat assumed that because I was a B.Ed. who had already had plenty of experience teaching physical education in a mainstream comprehensive school, whatever I offered in my teaching would provide everything a child might need. This was not the first occasion on which I had heard the term 'clumsy child', but now two experts — a doctor and a physiotherapist — were referring to it as a medical condition. Still, I did not anticipate that my previous assumptions as to what the word 'clumsy' meant in that context would need a great deal of modification. Experience and further research, however, as one might expect, soon began to show that 'clumsiness' was much more complicated than had appeared at first sight, and merely uncovered more and more ground, hitherto only patchily mapped, which needed to be examined in much more detail.

I soon realized that what people meant by clumsiness was actually 'delayed motor development' (DMD), a subject which I, like everyone else, had studied at my college of physical education, but which had not made a great deal of impact at the time. Indeed, because of my training, I thought that the progress of a child's sound motor development should be a natural spin-off from the activities in which he/she was asked to take part. But now, confronted for the first time with the physical development of children under the age of 11, I found that these assumptions were beginning to lose some of their credibility, and in consequence I felt a need to investigate the problem further.

I was surprised to find that there were no national statistics available. The physiotherapists I consulted, however, were of the opinion that as many as seven out of ten children in special schools, and possibly three out of any ten children in mainstream schools, suffer some impairment in their motor development. A national one-day conference held on November 12 1986, at the University of London Institute of Education, had in attendance many doctors, teachers, educational advisers and physiotherapists, who strongly supported this view.

What then are the negative effects upon children of delays in their motor development? To look at the question at its most basic level, they may be failing constantly in their day-to-day activities, because the ability to sit, stand, move easily, write or concentrate for lengthy periods is crucial in the learning situation. Constant failure will have an extremely damaging effect on self-esteem and self-confidence, both essential if children are to develop their potential to the full. So, correct motor development is vital for every child, for the ability to take exercise, and enjoy it, will have tremendous benefits for academic development as well as the obvious social benefits normally associated with physical education; and we may add to these the health arguments in favour of taking physical exercise. Too many children have cardio-vascular problems caused by modern living. Recent studies have indicated an abnormal build-up of cholesterol in the arteries of large numbers of 15-year-old children, and personal exercise, it goes without saying, will have a significant effect on weight control/obesity and decrease the need for artificial stimulants.

No one, however should underestimate the important part that good motor development will have on a child's ability to learn. It takes physical effort on a wide scale to sit still, receive instruction and act upon it; tasks which a child is asked to repeat time and time again. How, for example, can a child with very poor muscle tone and poor fine motor control manage to write? What chance is there of any child concentrating on instructions when he/she finds it physically uncomfortable to sit up straight, due to an extremely mobile pelvic girdle? The benefit to the whole child then is immense, provided due importance is given to all aspects of the child's development, and to this end I shall try to explain how to construct a plan which will ensure that, as far as possible, each child has an opportunity to achieve his or her individual potential. Perhaps equally important will be my attempt to show that such a plan need not fall victim to that ever present bugbear, the Timetable. 'I'm sorry, it cannot be done', 'we can't fit it in', 'we haven't the resources', 'we don't have the specialist help' — none of these excuses will stand. It can be done by anyone. This book will explain how.

One further point is worth consideration. We already have in place the 1981 Education Act with its far-reaching implications for the placement of children with special needs in their local main-stream schools; in addition, we now have the National Curriculum. Physical education must not be found wanting in meeting the challenges of such legislation. We need to produce solid arguments and workable schemes so that the subject can take its rightful place in the curriculum of all schools. People outside the profession: politicians, parents, governors, must be able to see clearly why it is there, and know what its benefits will be. Only by convincing parents and children brought up in an age where society is tending to move away from competitive organized sport within and across schools, to armchair video entertainment, that sound physical development is an essential tool in enabling them to progress in more diverse academic and social areas, shall we be able to win a battle, let alone the war.

Chapter 1

Aspects of Motor Development

Causes of Delay in Motor Development

The way the body normally develops complete motor control follows a clear pattern. Two things happen simultaneously:

    a. the infant gains control of his/her head and gradually extends this control down towards the feet;

    b. he/she gains control over the middle of his/her body and works this control outwards.

In the course of normal development, the infant becomes able to stabilize gross uncoordinated movements, refining them into more specific movements. Clearly then, he/she must experience certain specific areas of movement. These are:

    i. the coordination of large body movements which precede precise movements — such as throwing, catching and writing. (We can see therefore, that the large muscle will precede small muscle development).

    ii. bilateral movements, typical in young infants, leading to the development of unilateral movements. (These ultimately give a base upon which to build cross-lateral movement e.g., walking and running).

So in this normal pattern, development of complete motor control occurs in a continuous and uniform manner, at a rate particular to each individual.

Figure 1.1 Wobbly Man

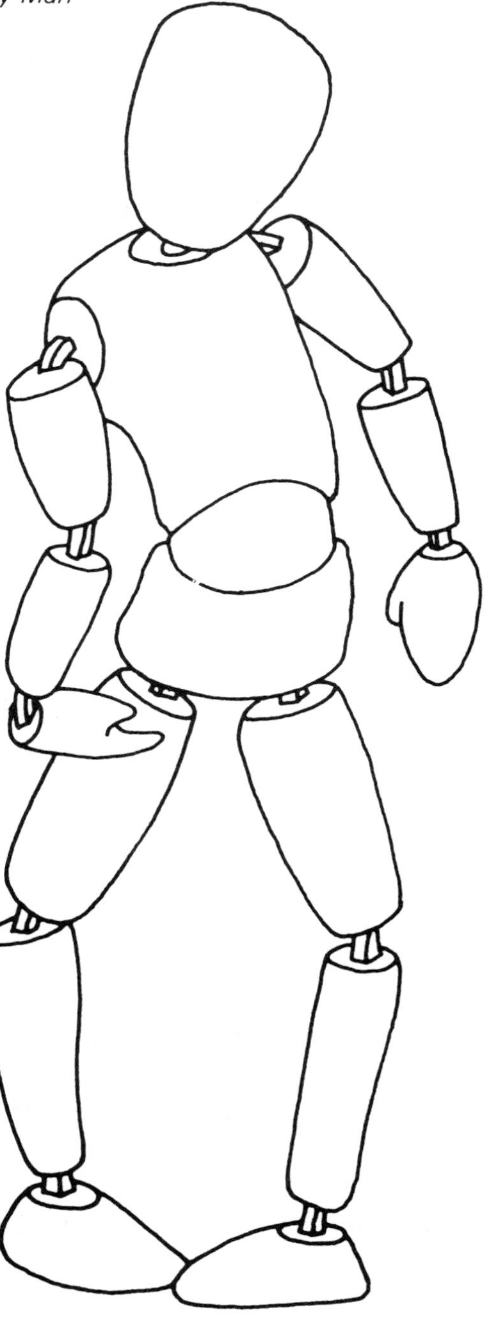

But what happens when bodies go wrong? For one thing, they find great difficulty in developing both muscle tone and muscle strength. For another, they may be unable to fixate properly at the joints, which means that they will appear to be double jointed. As a result of all three difficulties the child will be unable to grip or manipulate items which require the use of the fine muscles of the body, and will also develop an unwieldy gait in his/her day-to-day movement.

So now let us ask *why* some bodies do not develop motor control. There are several physiological areas which can influence and impair motor development — for example, the process of myelination, the primary reflexes, muscle excitation/inhibition or muscle tone. (There is also evidence that the development of motor control can be affected at the foetal stage. As far as this work is concerned, however, we will restrict ourselves to post-natal development). Let us look at each of these in more detail.

Myelination

Myelin is a sheath of fatty material which surrounds the neurons of certain fibres. Electrical impulses can jump across the gap in the neurons much more quickly when this sheath is present. Fibres covered in the thickest myelin sheath for example, can carry such impulses at 150 metres per second, whereas uncovered fibres can manage a speed of only 3 metres per second. Myelination is the process which coats the nerve axons in the fatty sheath of myelin. The deposition of myelin along the nerves, into the spinal cord, and eventually into the brain, begins at birth and continues into a child's late teens. This enables the electrical impulses to be delivered speedily to the appropriate body part. Any delay in the myelination process, either through disease or nutritional interference (key amino acids may be missing as a result of poor nourishment), can lead to permanent retardation. However, once myelin begins to deposit around the axons, it continues to be deposited rapidly.

Phasic Reflexes

Reflexes are automatic responses to stimuli which may not require any communication with the brain. Infants from nought to 2 months of life are dominated by the phasic reflexes which emanate from the spinal cord. Such reflexes are breathing, rooting (for mother's breast), digesting food, eliminating body-wastes, sneezing, hiccuping and coughing. At 2 to 4 months the dominant reflexes begin to emanate from the spinal cord and brain stem, and at this point the child is beginning to establish head control. From 6 months to 1 year there is an increase in the control of reflexes, mainly in the mid-brain area. These are known as primary reflexes. It is the ability of these higher primary reflexes to dominate the phasic reflexes which is important in gaining motor control. With increasing cortical control comes the ability to perform more complicated motor responses. Therefore any injury or defect which affects the central nervous system, especially the brain, while in utero or in birth, will produce serious problems for primary reflex dominance, and therefore motor control.

Muscle Tone

Sometimes referred to as muscle tension, muscle tone is of major importance during the early stages of developing motor control. It is dependent upon the balance between excitation and inhibition of muscle fibres. The result of too little inhibition is a condition known as hypertonia, (the muscles display a steel-like rigidity), whereas too little excitation leads to hypotonia, the principal cause of the 'floppy baby' syndrome. Those children seriously brain injured will exhibit both extremes of the condition, while children with Down's Syndrome will display hypotonia throughout their lives. Weak muscle tone is common in 'clumsy' children and these abnormalities in tonus can stem from a wide variety of defects in the brain, spinal cord or muscle itself.

Muscle development is thus a continuous battle of the higher cerebral reflexes over the primary reflexes. Again the message is clear:

if we wish to develop children's minds, no matter how limited their intelligence, motor control will play a significant part in assisting that process. So let us now turn to the components of motor control and try to see how an appreciation of the part each of these has to play in the total process will enable us to find a framework upon which our future work may be built.

The Components of Efficient Motor Function

I start with the simple question: what is efficient motor function? The physiotherapists have broken this down into ten distinct components.

1. Symmetrical activity.
2. Basic body movement.
3. Large muscle development.
4. Fine muscle development.
5. Eye-hand coordination.
6. Eye-foot coordination.
7. Body image.
8. Balance.
9. Rhythm.
10. Space and direction.

To make plain the part played by each of these, separately and together, in the programmes which follow, we shall now look at each one in more detail. In this way, I hope, the importance of each to the child's overall development will start to become clear.

1. Symmetrical Activity

Some children do not manage to establish the difference between the right and left sides of the body. This can be caused by the parents insisting that one side should receive preferential emphasis — 'write with the right hand and not with the left' is a well known social directive. Our bodies are structured so that we are designed symmetrically. Development of both sides of the body, rather than just one, is necessary, because this obviously leads to greater efficiency of movement and balance.

2. Basic Body Movement

When children are able to move skilfully and freely, their minds will also be free to interpret information relayed to them from their surroundings. Training in basic body movement provides them with the ability to play games and take part in activities. Through movement, children learn further about their environment, their bodies and the body's relationship with space and direction.

3. Large Muscle Development

Large muscle activities start children towards the development of their bodies for later life. This strengthening of the muscles around the pelvic and shoulder girdles in particular, helps them to be able to carry out their daily tasks with vigour and alertness. The emotional stresses placed on children in school situations can be better met if they have a strong body.

4. Fine Muscle Development

During the pre-school years, children develop hand-muscle control in a rather aimless manner, and therefore many children are deficient in the area of fine muscle and hand dexterity. It is important for children to develop individual strength, finger coordination, and to begin their symmetrical training in the use of both hands. There are also procedures for helping children who have difficulty in tracking objects with their eyes — another important area for fine muscle development.

5. Eye-hand Coordination

The combination of eyes and hands working together is necessary for the achievement of many tasks and experiences. Many children lack the ability visually to steer their hands through space to accomplish an appointed task.

6. Eye-foot Coordination

Children must be able to control the movement and direction of their bodies by using their legs and feet to the greatest advantage. Children need to be provided with experiences designed to correlate visual steering with movement of the feet.

7. Body Image

Children need to discover how their bodies move; they have to be able to sort out, that is to distinguish, one part of their body from another. We know that children start to develop an awareness of their bodies during infancy. So that this awareness can be developed to the highest degree, they need regular activities. If children develop a good image of their bodies, they will have a sound base to build perceptual skills which will be needed in future classroom activities.

8. Balance

Balance is the ability to sustain control of the body when using both sides simultaneously, individually or alternately. This involves transference of weight forwards, backwards and sideways. The ability to balance is essential to all locomotive tasks. If children have good balance, their bodies can act in an integrated manner, freeing their minds to concentrate on abstract matters.

9. *Rhythm*

Rhythm is a movement in flow. The development of rhythm can help children develop coordinated body management.

10. *Space and Direction*

After developing the awareness of body image, children must be able to identify their body position relative to their surroundings. They must be able to plan and execute an efficient course of action when moving from one position to another. The children's awareness of space and direction helps them to read from left to right — in Europe and America at least — and to form letters in an organized way.

Putting the Components Together

The complexity of children's physical development is actually a major part of the problem, and in many schools this development is taking place in children up to the age of 11 without the presence of any specialist physical education input. Perhaps this, in itself, helps to account for some of the prevalent figures for delayed motor development (see Introduction, pp. viii–ix).

Now that the component parts of efficient motor function have been identified, let me begin to put them together in a meaningful way. The ten components can be thought of as a group of children's building bricks and the child's body as a sort of pyramid. With every component in its proper place the pyramid is strong, well balanced, symmetrical and aesthetically pleasing. What would happen if any one of these bricks were removed? The shape would certainly be altered; its strength, its balance, symmetry and beauty might be affected. The removal might make only a minor difference, but equally might well result in the total collapse of the structure.

So far, so obvious. But now let us begin to visualize these bricks as the ten components of efficient motor function, and begin to remove first one, then another, from the pyramid. Take away

Figure 1.2 Pyramid of Motor Development

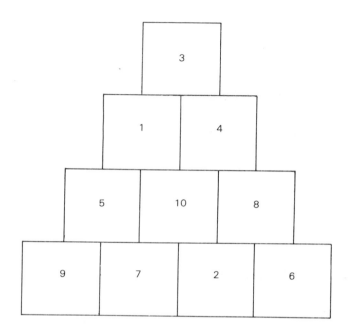

number ten for example — awareness of space and direction. Children with poor awareness would not suffer from any obvious defect in themselves, but the want could cause them several problems whilst in locomotion. However, removal of a further function, for example number five — eye-hand coordination, would cause intensification of their problems, for they would discover any racquet or ball game virtually beyond their capabilities.

Notice that we are not yet talking about any visible physical defect in the children, and their inability to do certain things may not be obvious at once in the multifarious activity of day-to-day living. So let us remove another function, for example number three — large muscle development. Without good muscle strength and girdle control, something as simple as sitting still becomes a struggle. Children will continually have to shift in their seats while trying to perform a task with their eyes and hands in a room where they are unsure how their bodies relate to the fixtures around them. We now have children with real problems because, certainly by this stage their pyramid is on the verge of collapse, if it has not given way already. (It is possible, of course, for children to suffer further with regard to efficient motor function, but with each additional malfunction, the handicap would become more physically obvious).

The children indeed, are probably feeling rather like pyramids — tottering to the point of falling down altogether. Concentration on a task for any length of time is, for them, virtually impossible and their continual fidgeting is likely to be misconstrued as inattentive behaviour. Now here are what really are clumsy children and (according to present modes of thinking) the appropriate response to their condition is to refer them, via their general practitioner, to a physiotherapist.

Signs of a Clumsy Child

The problem for any children labouring under such difficulties, is that there is no respite for them. Their problem will, and does, affect all aspects of their daily lives. They may arrive in school, full of frustration, already daunted and depressed by their struggles with those tasks which have to be done at home — the sheer hard work involved in dressing themselves, awkward buttons, zips and laces; the need to raise the arms above shoulder level, very difficult for such children; gettings legs into trousers; and the frustration of how much time this all takes. Breakfast exposes the lack of fine muscle control: utensils need to be gripped firmly if they are to cut or ladle or stir. They will often revert to tearing with the fork as they are unable to cut with a knife. Jugs of heavy liquid are aimed in the general direction of cups and plates, but often miss. Climbing up or down stairs can be painstaking and laborious. Parents begin to share the frustrations of their children, and it is no surprise that this frustration, felt by both sides, often spills over into loss of temper. On arrival at school, the children will be in no mood to cope with any more failure.

So, when they come in front of us in the classroom, what are the signals which may lead us to think we have 'clumsy' children on our hands? The most obvious sign will be their handwriting. The formation of letters is a difficult fine motor skill and even with continued practice, little progress will be made by 'clumsy' children. Such children may appear better when allowed to draw and will express a preference for this. However, there will be little in the way of fine detail and their drawings of body images may miss out arms and legs, and where they are present, they will fail to connect in the right place, if at all.

'Clumsy' children have poor muscle strength generally. They may have a constant need to fidget around in their seats or get up and walk around. They find it virtually impossible to sit still at their desks and concentrate for any length of time. And, to make things worse, they are probably not sure whether they are right or left handed.

As a classroom teacher, one must look for signs such as these. However, one must also bear in mind that each sign, taken alone, does not necessarily indicate a 'clumsy' child. Children may fidget because they are too hot or too cold or simply inattentive; they may have poor handwriting because they have been badly taught, or are too eager to get their words on to paper. But when several signs appear together, they may well be a signal of some degree of motor impairment, and under these circumstances, one would be well advised to begin to consult other colleagues who teach that child.

An ideal situation to make clearer observations on specific physical weaknesses, either alone or in combination, is presented when children are involved in a physical education lesson with you or maybe the school specialist. When such children have to dress and undress for PE, they stand out very clearly. Not only do they have problems with buttons, zips and laces, but they also seem to use a lot of energy getting arms and legs in and out of trousers and jumpers (a task they will already have been through at home). Weakness around the shoulder girdle makes it difficult for them to raise their arms above their heads and forces them to wrestle their way into vests, shirts and jumpers. Weakness in the muscles around the pelvic girdle means that the instant one foot is raised from the floor, 'wobbles' will set in, and an ordinary pair of trousers turns into a moving target. All these problems take a lot of energy and a lot of time, which invariably means that the 'clumsy' child is the last person to join the lesson. The one sure fire way to damage your self-esteem and sour relationships with your peers is by keeping them waiting or holding back their progress or slowing down their fun. Peer groups can be extremely severe on those who fail regularly and a 'clumsy' child will be one of the first to feel the full force of peer group rejection.

When the lesson begins, 'clumsy' children will have problems with many activities, especially where balancing on one leg is required, e.g., striking a football, hopping, crossing benches or beams. Again this is a result of being weak in the pelvic girdle region. Activities which involve shoulder strength and ultimately arm strength will prove extremely difficult. A straightforward press-up will be extremely difficult to perform and will cause the elbows to appear double-jointed because they will bend inwards to meet one another. Any attempt at a handstand would result in a dramatic collapse. The children's poor body image means that before they can catch or kick a ball, they have to look for their hands and feet, and should catching and kicking require locomotion as well, their inability to judge space and direction causes them to keep on crashing into walls and people, or simply stop whenever they are unsure of where they are.

Since the type of work these children produce is poor in comparison with that of their peers, they are likely to throw up their hands and give in. In addition, because they are aware that the result of their efforts is often unsuccessful, they quickly lose any concentration. It is plain to see therefore, that many of the legitimate activities employed as part of PE programmes simply reinforce the feelings of failure which 'clumsy' children have. However, armed with the knowledge of the components of efficient motor function, we should be able to recognize these children and begin to reorganize ourselves to tackle their problems. But should we fail to observe and act upon the many signals we have looked at, we cannot possibly begin to alleviate the tensions within 'clumsy' children, and we will have to accept either that 'acting out' and boisterous behaviour will become an integral part of their survival and avoidance skills, or that they may simply opt out altogether and retire within themselves. There are many ways in which such children can be helped, but these can be brought into play only if we all become alert to two important points: (a) the need for all children to have a sound physical base to their existence, and (b) that all adults who meet such 'clumsy' children have a part to play in improving their lot, no matter how minor the difficulties may appear to be.

Chapter 2

Existing Programmes for the DMD Child

Delayed motor development is not actually a new idea because various people have developed schemes to try to deal with it. These schemes are aimed at different groups with different problems. For example, Veronica Sherbourne, Walli Meier and the Halliwick Swimming Method have all designed programmes for the profoundly disabled; the physiotherapists and the Child Development Centres for children diagnosed as 'clumsy'; more conventional programmes such as the Southern Counties AA 'Ten Step' Award Scheme for the able-bodied. My experience with all of these has suggested to me that elements from all of them can be adapted for use with a whole range of children. This is a particularly important point and one which needs to be emphasized. 'Clumsy' is not synonymous with 'physically disabled'. That is a notion one really has to cast aside. A physically disabled person is precisely that — physically disabled, whereas 'clumsiness' is largely a state of mind. Teachers perceive children as 'clumsy'; children perceive themselves as 'clumsy'. So 'clumsiness' is to a great extent a psychological condition which has certain physical consequences, rather than the other way round. This is not to say that medical problems have nothing to do with it, simply that the condition is very often more psychological than physical.

In consequence, when you devise a scheme of work for 'clumsy' children, you must adapt it to suit the children you actually have in front of you, and this means that you must be prepared to be flexible in your perception of those children's needs. *Adaptability* should be your key word. What I intend to do now is to describe the various schemes I mentioned above — (a) to explain what their particular aims are, and (b) to suggest how elements in those programmes can be adapted to any of the whole range of 'clumsy' children.

Veronica Sherbourne

Veronica Sherbourne was trained in physical education, physio-therapy and the methods of Rudolph Laban. She has had more than twenty-five years experience of looking at movement, and of observing the ways others have gone about teaching it. In recent years she has turned her attention largely to children who are severely retarded and has developed a technique which not only benefits them but also has implications for the physical development of all children, regardless of their movement ability.

She begins with the notion that motor control emanates from the brain and spinal cord. Therefore, the starting point must be the trunk because it is there that heightened awareness can be best achieved. The common belief is that gross motor development underpins fine motor development and, in consequence, increased stimulation of the abdominal region should give a base upon which to increase the individual's awareness of his/her body. Increased stimulation increases bodily awareness; therefore the common belief is true.

Children with severe handicaps would appear to have two pre-requisites for making significant physical progress:

    i. a need to improve their self-awareness and body-image, and

    ii. a need to develop an awareness of others, in other words, the ability to make meaningful relationships.

It is important to note however that these concepts apply equally well to all children.

Now let us turn to working out these concepts in specific programmes. When trying to develop and enhance self-awareness and expand that awareness to others, it is essential that we keep uppermost in our minds the value of multi-sensory input. Young children find it difficult to focus their attention inwards and it is therefore necessary to use exercises which will involve their trunk and body parts in a lot of sensory activity. Activities which involve rolling, falling and transferring weight across different body parts are excellent for the abdominal region of the body, but should be carried out at a level which causes no unnecessary discomfort. In other words, a low-level approach is best because at that level the child feels secure and one can then begin to build upon that foundation of trust. Patting knees, rubbing feet, squashing fingers and tickling the trunk are additional means of providing sensory input, and it is useful to get the child to name the part of the body which is being stimulated. Every child will respond to such input and reinforcement.

Locomotion is the next stage. Here you are trying to get the child moving up and down and sideways, and in different directions at gradually increasing speeds. So activities such as crawling, kneeling, squatting and jumping can be introduced where appropriate. Notice that it is essential to provide a firm structure for each session, and to get the children to repeat each element, so that motor development is reinforced and progress made.

Where it can be arranged, the most powerful aid to progress for developmentally delayed children is the input of a more able adult or older child. Such relationship play is invaluable in extending the movement vocabulary of children. It is important that the activities on offer are within the scope of all present and that the senior partner is able to exert a degree of flexible control over situations. Relationship play, however, must have a tight structure for it to be truly valuable.

Each session should provide opportunities for all children to become aware of the focus of their own strength by, for example, pushing or pulling against their partner. They should also be given a chance to share the flow of movement initiated by someone else. If they sit in their partner's lap and their partner rocks from side to side, the movement is coming from the older source but involving the young recipient in its action. Relaxation is another important element of the lesson, although it must be borne in mind that a successful session consists of all these elements and will take the child through a wide, not a narrow, range of physical experiences. The aim of working with a partner is to bring about a mutual trust, to encourage all the children to be willing to let their partner control their bodies. In making partners work against each other we are hoping that the less able child will be able to experience the feeling, sustain that feeling, and not have that feeling destroyed by the partner. This is why share or flow relationships are important, and exercises such as rocking and swinging will help to reinforce mutual dependence and trust. Wherever possible, partners should of course swap roles — and this is where the two-way interaction greatly benefits the more able partner, because, when testing the younger ones, they themselves must find the correct levels on which to operate. In other words, they must become teacher as well as play friend.

In my experience, one of the most frequent observations to come out of INSET days is, 'This has been very interesting and very useful but, after all, we are adults from different establishments and so it has been relatively easy for us to create a one-to-one working relationship under these conditions. How am I going to manage to recreate that when I get back to my school?'. I shall offer practical suggestions in the second half of this book to help overcome this difficulty; for the moment just let me indicate what we have been able to do in Cambridge.

We started by mixing children in our own school, and then extended this to include children from two comprehensives, two junior schools, one infant school and two schools for children with severe learning difficulties. The teachers who are involved in all this are unanimous in their view of the benefits which children gain from working in this way. On a purely physical level, their body awareness and physical performance improves all round; their self-esteem and self-confidence are greatly enhanced, and — a very important point — the activities provide a great deal of fun! The older children, too, derive specific benefits from their involvement in this process, for they seem to strike up positive relationships with those put under their care, relationships which are most important both for them and their charges. Children from mainstream schools with apparent special educational needs especially seem to benefit from this type of involvement. I shall return to this point later, see pp. 104–5.

Walli Meier

Although there are striking similarities between the work of Walli Meier and that of Veronica Sherbourne, both of whom have a common aim, if you attend a course run by either of them you will notice that they adopt very different approaches towards their students. The more extrovert and dynamic personality of Walli Meier and her strong sense of a *psychological* approach to the attitudes of surrounding movement give yet another valuable dimension to one's work with children who suffer from delayed motor development. She continually strives to build within each child a vocabulary of body parts, body movements and body images which is meant to enable the child to interpret its whole body in a more meaningful way.

Walli Meier has a clear belief that how we manage ourselves physically manifests itself psychologically, i.e., the ability to control your body will not only make you physically 'firm' but also psychologically 'firm'. In more precise terms, if you are more likely to have the whole of your body under control, then, in addition, you will increase your capacity for psychological — i.e., self — control. As in Sherbourne's system, the centre of the body is seen as the fulcrum of solid physical development, although Meier's approach at times comes from the opposite end of the scale, i.e., fine motor through to gross motor (see Figure 2.1).

Aggression and tension are seen as qualities which should be developed in a positive way. Children who are incapable of exerting such qualities should be a cause for concern, because these are the children who will ultimately give in, and they must be encouraged to promote their own sense of 'self'. Without this sense of 'self' they may find they exclude themselves from affection, the ability to share their space with others, and, in consequence, they may ultimately be unable to initiate affection themselves either verbally or physically. So time should be spent during each session boosting that sense of 'self', and encouraging exhibitions of affection. This can be done by claiming spaces, stating names — 'My name is David and I have a right to be here!' — adopting positions of strength, projecting oneself verbally, cuddling, massaging, tickling and touching.

Ultimately we have to build trust. We must be able to let go of

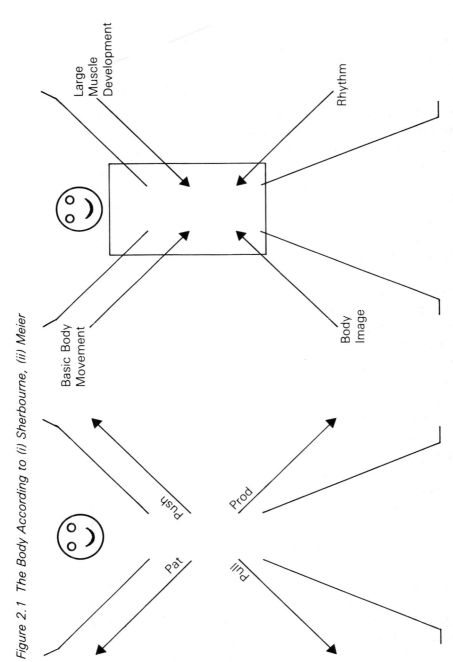

Figure 2.1 The Body According to (i) Sherbourne, (ii) Meier

Poor connections in the body centre prevent correct movement signals from reaching out to the rest of the body.

our own body and let someone else take control — not something which can be done if you cannot relax and not an easy task for many adults, let alone children.

As I have already intimated, body image is central to the way in which Walli Meier works. The need to identify body parts and understand how they move, where they move and with what they connect, she thinks is of great importance. To emphasize this, she is very keen on the use of music in her lessons. She gives much attention to detail: for example, stepping begins at the heel, goes on to the ball of the foot, and ends with the toe. Walli Meier's exercise, however, reverses the process in order to draw attention to the component parts of this apparently simple movement. What this illustrates is her belief that movements flow from specific centres such as the joints and so her exercises are designed to focus the child's attention (a) on where the centre itself is, (b) what the centre itself can do, and (c) what other movements can be extended from it. Hands clench into fists and extend through to the fingertips via each joint. Elbows break, wrists roll, backs curve, arms swing and so on. (Here we can see clear links with the components of efficient motor function, which I listed earlier).

It is also important for the child to realize that movements can be developed in different ways. Their speed can be altered — fast, andante, slow; so can their direction — forward, backward, left or right; so can their level — low, medium, high. All these changes involve energy and so a realization that different types of movement require different amounts of energy is made possible, and here music can be used to very good effect. The idea is that all children should mobilize as much of their body as they can and make that mobility function as efficiently as possible, and this in turn should lead to a reduction of physically related stress or tension.

Walli Meier, then, is a strong advocate, first, of establishing what she sees an an all-important control over the centre of the body in order to bring to life an area which previously had been unstable; and secondly, of relationship play, in order to advance not only physical development, but also social awareness and an ability in all children to make available to others their own personal space.

As I said at the beginning of this section, the techniques of Walli

Meier and Veronica Sherbourne are very similar. Where they differ is in the way they perceive the centre of the body. Veronica Sherbourne sees this area as stagnant or lifeless, and therefore in need of being re-vivified: Walli Meier sees it as essentially unstable (she actually uses the word 'floppy' to describe it), and therefore in need of being brought under control. In consequence their approaches to the solution of the problem differ.

Nevertheless, a combination of aspects of their approaches can be very effective. They represent, to some extent, opposite ends of the spectrum of disability. Veronica Sherbourne tends to deal with the profoundly handicapped, whereas Walli Meier tends to concern herself with those whose movement vocabulary is diminished not by profound handicap but by delayed motor development, or 'clumsiness', or by psychological disturbance. A practical way of using what they have to offer is to assess the type and degree of disability of individual children, assess too — a most important point — their range of ability, and then select those exercises of both Veronica Sherbourne and Walli Meier which will best answer their needs.

The Halliwick Method

This method, which is concerned specifically with the teaching of swimming, aims to show the physically disabled how they can become independent of others by relying upon the natural buoyancy of water; and the most important factor in its success is that one-to-one relationship between teacher and pupil which, as we have seen before, needs to be built up during the initial stages of instruction. Because of the necessity for such a relationship, such intensive use of manpower so to speak, the Halliwick Method has been used most widely in special clubs and in schools which deal specifically with the physically handicapped and can therefore call upon the services of a wide range of adults such as teachers, welfare assistants, care assistants, physiotherapists and volunteers.

When it comes to 'clumsy' children, however, the situation is somewhat different because 'clumsy' children, who have tremendous

Table 2.1 from Martin (1981)

The Halliwick Method is based upon known scientific principles of hydrodynamics and body mechanics. The development takes place in ten stages, grouped into four phases:		
Phase 1	Mental adjustment Disengagement	Adjustment to water
Phase 2	Vertical Rotations Lateral Rotation Combined Rotation	Rotations
Phase 3	Upthrust Balance Turbulent Gliding	Control of movement in the water
Phase 4	Simple Progression Basic Progression	Movement in water

problems with their physical movement on dry land, usually transfer those problems into water and then add another problem — fear of water itself. Clearly, the opportunity for each swimmer to have his/her own individual instructor, however, will help in large measure to deal with that initial fear.

Moreover, the social interaction that evolves from such a relationship is invaluable. The swimmers have a constant supply of unobtrusive personal attention, and with the aid of human support (which is much more responsive and easier to decrease than artificial flotation) they can learn to come to terms with their balance in the water, effective breathing and, through a variety of games, begin to learn about and enjoy the properties of water. The enormous gap, which is usual in swimming lessons, between the poolside instructor and the group of swimmers is here largely eliminated, with the result that water confidence advances much more rapidly. Children who previously felt awkward and restricted on dry land enter realms of mobility alien to their current experience: and if any of the swimmers are disabled, it may in fact lead to their first real experience of free and independent movement.

It is also worth noting that fifth formers who have taken the role of instructors and assisted me with 'clumsy' children in the pool have needed to produce skills, particularly in their use of language and touch, with which they felt uncomfortable initially. The consequent change in their attitudes, confidence and belief in their role has to be seen to be fully appreciated. This is reflected in the responsibility and reliability they now give to the programme, and in their seemingly endless ability to invent new ways to stimulate the interest and help build the confidence of the swimmer in their charge.

The techniques of the Halliwick Method are not something that I can attempt to describe fully. I myself attended a course run by the Association of Swimming Therapy and full details of this method and any proposed courses in your area can be obtained by contacting the Honorary Secretary, whose address is at the back of this book.

I should perhaps make two additional points. The first is that the Halliwick Method in itself is not intended to replace the swimming programme of any school, but to supplement what it already does for physically disabled and delayed motor development children. The second is that a non-specialist school may find it difficult to provide enough adults to implement the Halliwick programme. This, however, as I have indicated above, can be mitigated by using older children, especially fifth-formers who will derive much benefit from taking on the role of instructor under supervision.

The preparation of the fifth-year children, prior to working with the swimmers is most important; this is covered in Chapter 4, pp. 62–3. Without preparation they will not readily, nor safely, adopt the role of instructor and this will prove counter-productive.

Ten Step Award Scheme

The award presents us with 'a method of learning and practising basic physical skills'. Followed through to its conclusion, it sees itself as 'a test of individual skills for children of all abilities'. The varied activities offered by the programme readily fulfil many of the requirements listed in the components of efficient motor function.

The scheme operates along similar lines to the Amateur Athletic Association Five Star Awards Scheme. The children are given a number of points according to the time taken for a run, distance, and height or length of a jump. They add up their five highest scoring

Table 2.2 Ten Step Award Scheme

Activity	Components affected
Standing long jump Three spring jumps Seated soccer ball throw	Symmetrical movement, Rhythm, Body image, Large muscle development, Balance
Running Activities, e.g.: 50 metres and 75 metres 6 × 10 metres shuttle run Compass Run, Object pick-up race, 800 metres, and also 500 metres walk.	Basic body movement, Rhythm, Eye-hand coordination, Space and direction
40 metres Hurdles, Slalom run, Standing triple jump, 15 metres hopping, Running long-jump, 50 metres skipping, Cricket/Rounders ball throw, High jump, Standing soccer ball throw	Eye-foot coordination Space and direction Large muscle development Fine muscle development Rhythm Body image

events and will qualify for one of the step awards, starting with one step and culminating in the triple ten, which is the highest award.

The variety of activity on offer makes it fun for the children and when I was using it, I was able to adapt it in the following way. Throughout the Autumn and Spring terms, the children were put through a series of circuits which I devised in conjunction with the physiotherapist so that we could be sure they would meet their motor development needs. This seemed an ideal opportunity to give new dimension to their programme without losing sight of those needs. As you can see from Table 2.2, if you build an outdoor circuit which incorporates two activities from each group, by the time the children have finished, they will have experienced all the components they need to develop the whole range of motor functions. This is because *one* activity affects several components in some way; for example, standing long-jump affects:

    i. symmetrical movement
    ii. rhythm
    iii. body image

iv. large muscle development
v. balance.

The experience of learning, remembering and developing new outdoor circuits throughout the summer was every bit as rewarding for the children as their experience of the indoor circuits.

Two points are worth making: first, there is a certain amount of administration attached to all this should you wish to pursue the award scheme, and second, pursuing the awards is not necessary, but they do provide scope for further development of the summer scheme for *all* children under the age of 11, whether 'clumsy' or not.

Details of the whole scheme are available to all schools and are to be recommended for their objectivity, variety, adaptability and the fun they give the children. The added bonus is that you are unlikely to need to purchase any new equipment, since the human body is the major piece of apparatus.

Physiotherapists and the Child Development Centre

The role of the school physiotherapist and of the Child Development Centre in Cambridge were crucial in the introduction and advancement of the many varieties of activities used to help the children with delayed motor development in my school, and I owe much of the information which I have used in Chapter 1 to the work done by the physiotherapist who was in the school at that time. Both she and her colleagues at the Child Development Centre were convinced that a multidisciplinary approach by the professionals involved with children was essential. They were, however, fully aware of the limitations of their resources and were more than happy if teachers were capable of contributing to this aspect of their work. They also recognized that most teachers in the infant/junior/primary sector were often unclear (purely as a result of the training they themselves received) as to why sound physical development should be considered vital to the children's school life.

It is most important that physiotherapists and teachers should cooperate fully with each other, and acknowledge that they are dealing with a whole problem which needs a united, not a divided approach. This is not to say that their roles should be amalgamated, merely that each should play his/her part in awareness of a common goal.

The role of the physiotherapist within schools is clear. Where any child has been referred to his/her General Practitioner as possibly suffering from delayed motor development, an assessment must be carried out to establish where the deficiencies lie. The test currently favoured is the Test of Motor Impairment or TOMI, previously known as Stott Testing. This test is not a complicated one, but any large scale administration of it in a mainstream school would be an impossible task for a teacher. Some knowledge of how the test works, however, is probably useful. In Chapter 3, there are references to TOMI. It should be noted that when those tests were carried out under the old 'Stott Testing' system, the method of scoring was different from the modern TOMI.

If tests prove that a problem exists, the child will then be seen by the physiotherapist (once a week usually) for exercises which are aimed at remediating the problem. It seems essential to me that the teacher in charge of that child during any session of physical activity ought to be aware of any special requirements he/she may have. Therefore channels of communication in schools must be open to the support services; for example, in the case of junior schools, between the physiotherapist and classroom teacher.

The Child Development Centre offers another dimension to the treatment of children. Here they may work in peer groups, and also with therapists other than the physiotherapist, and this can help with their dressing, undressing and various other social skills. Several visits to a Child Development Centre led me to think that the type of work done there could also be done in school, with suitable modifications, of course. Children diagnosed as 'severely clumsy' are often taken out of school and sent to such a Centre, and in many cases make a dramatic improvement. Frequently indeed, they do not complete the recommended full six months because they improve to the point where they ought to rejoin their peers at school at an earlier stage. As you may imagine, Centres work under great pressure because of the

large numbers of children who are referred to them for their special-
ized treatment.

If the physiotherapy service is under such pressure, why do we
have to send such children out of school and to a hospital? Can we
not remediate these children in school? After all, we support poor
readers, we give extra help with mathematics, we run groups for non-
swimmers, we get help from speech therapists. Is it possible for us to
organize within school a programme to assist children who have real
difficulties in their physical development? Surely the answer is 'yes'.
However, there are one or two points which ought to be taken into
account. For example, the staff must be fully informed about the
benefits which will accrue for both children and teachers, because
they will be asked to release children from academic work. They may
also have to rethink the structure and content of physical education
they have been teaching. Above all they may need to re-evaluate
(completely) their notion of the significance of physical development
for the all-round well-being of their children. So administrative
problems involving timetable and INSET are likely to make an
appearance. Goodwill all round will minimize the difficulties, and
the results for all concerned will make everyone's efforts well worth-
while.

The eight photographs which follow illustrate the ways in which,
during the type of sessions described in Chapter 2, children pass
through the stages of making initial contact, forming individual
relationships, and, finally, taking a full part in group work.

Illustration 2.1: First contact

Illustration 2.2: Pushing the rock

Illustration 2.3: All pull together

Illustration 2.4: Trust

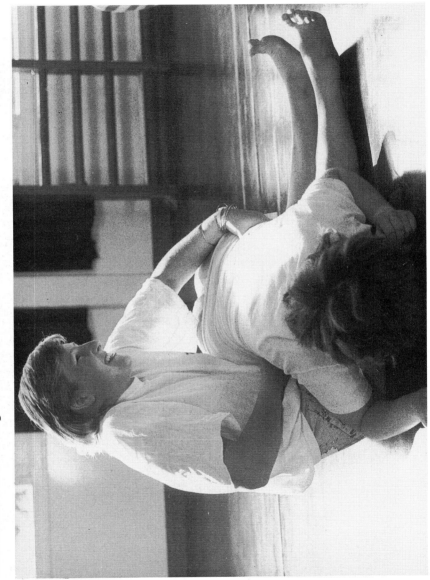

Illustration 2.5: Tickling is fun

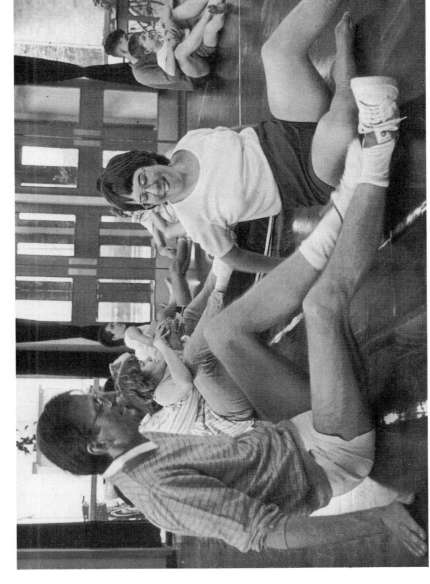

Illustration 2.6: The prisoner escapes

Illustration 2.7: The competitive spirit

Illustration 2.8: End of session

Chapter 3

Some Case Histories

Cooperation between school and specialists is important, but it is equally important that it be informed cooperation. Each person involved must understand, in some measure at least, what it is that the other is trying to do, otherwise one runs the risk of having several people ostensibly working for the benefit of the child, but conducting their work in isolation from each other. Too many specialists spoil the broth! This indeed has been my own experience and will probably sound familiar to many.

So let me now explain briefly what is likely to happen if a delayed motor development child is referred to a physiotherapist. The physiotherapist will want to discover whether the child's development is delayed by any known medical condition, such as spasticity, cerebral palsy or spina bifida. If no ascertainable physical problem exists, she is then likely to administer tests, such as the Test of Motor Impairment (TOMI), which will diagnose more precisely areas of poor motor development. Finally, the physiotherapist will compile a report which not only gathers together all the facts she has been able to discover, but will also include guidelines for treatment. Children eventually seen by physiotherapists are evidently in a bad way. These are not *all* the 'clumsy' children in the school; they are just *some* of the 'clumsy' children in the school.

The best way of explaining what this can mean in practice is to look at individual cases, and there follow four case studies with which I hope to illustrate how important it is for the schools and physiotherapists to come together to produce more effective guidelines for treatment. As we already know, where no link exists between school and physiotherapist, options for treatment are limited to:

a. Individual treatment plus parental input,
b. Group sessions at the Child Development Centres (where they exist).

Individual treatment may take place in the school or at home, once or twice a week. (The group session option will almost certainly be once a week only). The physiotherapist will want to emphasize strongly that delayed motor development children derive more benefit from frequency rather than length of activity. Twenty minutes of such activity per day are better than one hour a week. The sheer volume of work physiotherapists have to undertake means, however, that because they are more or less limited to the options mentioned above, progress is somewhat delayed, and the stigma of being withdrawn for treatment on a one-to-one basis in school continues to pose problems for 'clumsy' children with regard to their image and esteem. In consequence, they may exhibit boisterous behaviour or indifference to the treatment.

The case studies are close versions of actual physiotherapist's reports presented to a teacher and I have appended comments of my own at the end of each, so that you can see how teachers can contribute to the process and help to overcome some of the difficulties which a physiotherapist on her own inevitably faces.

Case A: Donald, aged 13 years.
Medical problem: Hemiplegia (left side).

Donald presents as very immature for his age, and he likes to appear very outgoing and sociable. However, when the pressure is applied academically or by peers, he simply crumbles, as would a very young child. His recording skills are poor in comparison with his peers, and he seems to be forever catching up. He will seek approval from peers by misbehaving in formal situations, and becomes confused when he is left 'carrying the can'.

Main problems:
1. Difficulty with weight-bearing through the left side.
2. Poor balance.

3. Poor hand–eye/foot–eye coordination.
4. Reluctance to take part in two-handed or left-handed activities.
5. General stiffness, and inability to use left side properly.

Guidelines for activities:
   a. In all positions make sure that Donald is weight-bearing equally through left and right sides. Encourage weight transference forwards and backwards or side to side.
   b. Balance work in standing, kneeling and on hands and knees.
   c. Ball work — throwing, catching and kicking. Be sure to work with both hands and both feet.
   d. Any activity which involves the use of both hands, e.g., pushing, pulling, holding.

Donald was also given a number of self-stretching exercises which he could go through in school or at home:

   i. Cross-legged sitting (left leg under right), push down on knees to stretch inner thighs.
   ii. Lying on his tummy, clasp hands and stretch forward along the floor.
   iii. Lying on tummy, bend left knee, then lift leg off the floor.

There were also activities which were to be discouraged, such as rushing around, because this increased abnormal movements in his affected side; using his right hand to the exclusion of his left; total reliance on others for the maintenance of his physical abilities.

Comments

The status quo for many delayed motor development children is to compartmentalize the treatment — i.e., the physiotherapist will treat them on an individual basis away from their peers. Unfortunately, the PE lesson will have been designed for their more able peers, and in consequence the delayed motor development child becomes more and more isolated, and less and less able to join everyone else in a normal lesson on something like equal terms. This consequence is not necessarily the physiotherapist's fault. It simply tends to work that way in practice. However, as soon as the channels of communication (for the support services within school) are opened, the information accumulated for such children has implications for these children throughout their school day. This, for example, is what I arranged for Donald:

  i. Once a week physiotherapy (to continue).
  ii. One small group session on a Monday to assist with self-stretching exercises.
  iii. He then joined a specialist delayed motor development peer group which had been formed to assist children from a local severe learning difficulty school, and which used many of the methods of Veronica Sherbourne and Walli Meier.

Notice that each of these options was an addition to, and not a replacement for, his normal PE programme of a swimming session, a movement session and a games-oriented session. My intentions were that Donald should increase the level of his physical activity, boost his motor development, experience increasing success and thereby enhance his own self-image and esteem. The results became evident as the months went by. There was a distinct improvement in his physical awareness and ability, and also a growing social confidence — most important to a young lad at this particular stage of his adolescent development.

Case B: Annabel, aged 11 years.
Medical problem: mild cerebral palsy.

Annabel handles her difficulties well. She is quiet but not introverted. She is capable of working hard but has very poor recording skills. This case is a particularly good example of a child who outwardly appears very normal, but because of her medical condition, exhibits her problems across a wide spectrum of her work in school.

Annabel was seen by both the physiotherapist and the occupational therapist. The physiotherapist was particularly concerned about the poor girdle strength throughout the body and felt that plenty of work should go into that area of her development because this would give her a base upon which to build. The occupational therapist suggested the following:

1. *Shoulder girdle stability*
   a. Ball games, particularly those which involve throwing over the head.
   b. Clasping hands together and hitting sponge ball away, as in volleyball.
   c. Games such as 'Simon Says'.
   d. Writing on a blackboard with small pieces of chalk.

2. *To improve tactile awareness of both hands*: (all played without vision)
   a. Feeling textures and naming them.
   b. 'What's in the Bag' game.
   c. Identifying shapes and objects by feel.
   d. Heavy/light object comparisons.
   e. Cold/warm object comparison.
   f. Arranging cups of different sizes.

3. *To improve manipulative skills*: (encourage use of both hands together)
   a. Plasticine.
   b. Cutting.
   c. Tearing.
   d. Baking.
   e. Kneading dough.
   f. Rolling out.

4. *Paper and pencil skills*:
   a. Use of small pieces of chalk or short pencil.
   b. Mazes.
   c. Dot to dot.

d. Holding templates and drawing round them.

e. Drawing lines across a large piece of paper to encourage her to cross the midlines of her body.

Comments

In this information, the emphasis is heavily in favour of fine motor development, sequencing and body image. As I said before, gross motor development underpins fine motor development; therefore other means had to be found to support her physical needs. Annabel arrived at the school at a time when a motor development group was already in existence. So what happened was as follows:

i. Annabel had an individual physiotherapy session each week.

ii. She also joined the motor development group which was small in number and had some vertical streaming.

ii. The classroom teacher produced work based on the information received from the occupational therapist.

This was in addition to the normal PE programme of swimming, movement and a games/sequencing lesson each week. Annabel was therefore benefitting from physical activity at least five times a week in her school. Although her condition poses problems, she is happy to participate fully in all these sessions. In fact they are now something to which she looks forward and at which she is increasingly more successful.

Both Donald and Annabel were originally more easily identifiable because they suffered from clear medical conditions. The 'clumsy' child can be far more difficult to spot and many of the signs have been highlighted in Chapter 1. Case C is a good example of a young girl with a general physical development way below her chronological age, who is very quiet, introverted and withdrawn and was first assessed by the physiotherapist when she was 8 years old.

Case C: Anne, aged 10 years.
Medical problem: none (eventually diagnosed as 'clumsy').

After being tested by the physiotherapist (using the Stott–Moyes–Henderson Test of Motor Impairment) Anne was found to be operating at a sub 5-year-old level. This is the lowest level which the test records. The school physiotherapist made the following observations:

Summary:
Her static balance is reasonable, but her dynamic balance is poor for her age. She has difficulty following and interpreting instructions, therefore this adds to her problems with motor planning. Her girdle fixation is poor and isolation movement is also poor. She has decreased spinal mobility.

Aims:
    a. Improve both static and dynamic balance.
    b. Improve weight transference.
    c. Increase muscle power of shoulder and pelvic girdles.
    d. Improve eye–hand/eye–foot coordination.
    e. Work on following instructions and copying sequences.

Comments

In fact, Anne was deficient in virtually every area listed in the components of efficient motor function, and was simply not functioning socially. Remediation was set up as follows:

    i. An individual session from the physiotherapist each week.
    ii. Anne joined the school motor development group.
    iii. Much more time was allocated by the classroom teacher, to observe and sequence things.

Again, none of this ran contrary to the existing PE programme on offer. The aim of more individual attention was to boost her confidence and her desire to play a fuller part in these other activities.

Case D: Sean, aged 13 years.
Medical problem: none (diagnosed as 'clumsy').

At first sight, the final case study seems to be the archetypal 'clumsy' child. It is a boy, by which I do not mean to imply that most 'clumsy' children are boys, but that 'clumsy' boys tend to be discovered more often than 'clumsy' girls. This is because the 'clumsy' boy is likely to be more extrovert. His boisterous, noisy, restive behaviour inevitably attracts the teacher's attention, and therefore any problems he has will come under scrutiny. At every conference I have attended, it has been said by someone that, statistically, boys are more likely to be 'clumsy' than girls. This, however, is an area which needs further investigation.

This particular boy, Sean, was noisy, emotionally overcharged, boisterous, and had set himself up as the class clown. Any tactic seemed legitimate if it helped to disguise his inabilities. He had managed to survive the whole of junior school without having begun to master the required reading, writing or mathematical skills. His referral happened at the same time as his being designated a child with special educational needs. This was very soon after he had started at his local comprehensive school. He was then about $11\frac{1}{2}$ years old.

Summary:
During assessment Sean appeared to have some difficulty with both gross and fine motor skills. His muscle power is generally decreased and his ability to fixate and isolate movements is poor. Weight transference tends to be difficult for him, and so his movements are somewhat stilted and laboured. His balance, both static and dynamic, is poor for his age.

When given a series of verbal commands in the form of an obstacle course, he was unable to follow more than two consecutive commands, although he understood the concepts of over, under, through, behind, etc. However, his motor planning and spatial awareness are very good. I felt he would benefit greatly from a course of physiotherapy and arranged to see him weekly at school, and talked to his PE teacher to see if some of the activities he needs could be incorporated into his PE lessons.

Aims of Treatment:
1. Increase muscle power generally — especially at shoulder and hip girdles.
2. Improve weight transference ability.
3. Improve balance, static and dynamic.
4. Work on posture copying — very important as he tends to work on visual clues.
5. Practise hand–eye / foot–eye coordination.

Guidelines for activities:
a. Rolling — with legs and arms straight to strengthen abdominals, also rolling in a blanket.
b. Muscle power — sit-ups, press-ups, straight leg raises, static quads exercises.
c. Four point kneeling — raise opposite arm and leg, resisted crawling.
d. Ball work — while kneeling, standing, half standing.
e. Jumping, hopping, standing on one leg and moving football with the other.
f. Imitating postures — 'Simon Says'-type games.
g. Following commands — build up number and complexity.

Comments

It is easy to see why, at $11\frac{1}{2}$ years old, Sean was experiencing difficulty in many areas of his school work. The disturbing aspect of all this is that he was allowed to continue for so long without this assessment taking place. It is children like Anne and Sean who are the most difficult to identify, yet they are among the most likely to succeed as a result of remediation.

Now as we have seen earlier, delayed motor development is not a problem which confines itself to only a few children with highly visible disabilities, such as severe physical handicap. The range of children with delayed motor development is very wide indeed, and therefore, one can expect to encounter this range, either in part or whole, within a single school.

In the four case studies above, I have tried to show briefly how, by altering the timetable and creating special groups with appropriate activities, the time given over to physical activity for such children can both benefit from the work of the physiotherapists and be used to support it; and I hope that an awareness of how and what physiotherapists report will give teachers the confidence to take an active part in implementing, and perhaps even adding to, the physiotherapists' input.

Chapter 4

Building a New Approach

The growing realization that delayed motor development is a problem, and quite a large problem too, has also revealed that current research and literature relating to this field of study is fairly limited. The latest book on the subject, *Graded Activities for Children with Motor Difficulties* by James Russell, was published in June 1988. Although Russell's opinions on the problem are the same as mine, our approaches to it are different. Whilst recognizing that 'prevention is preferable to remediation' (p. 11) for example, he clearly believes in the prescriptive approach. A problem exists; let us find not just one answer but several, if we can.

'If you have locked the door in your house and the key to that door has been lost, the greater the variety of keys you can collect to try and unlock the door, the more chance there is of finding one which will work' (p. 13). Now I do not disagree with that, but I lay much greater emphasis on the preventative aspect of the problem, an aspect not really treated by Russell.

One difficulty created by the purely prescriptive approach is that teachers commonly see delayed motor development as a specialist matter, and in my experience, the prescriptive approach to non-specialist teachers simply serves to reinforce their non-specialism and undermines their already shaky confidence.[1] The problem of the non-specialist teacher is one of time. For extreme cases of delayed motor development we can bring in the physiotherapist, but where do we find the time to work with those whose difficulties, although less obvious, are a definite restriction on their whole development?[2] We need to create for these children additional time in school — time to be spent on their physical development in order to enhance the work done by the support services, not replace it, and this extra time needs to be put to efficient use by the teacher.

But what of those who have slipped through the net? They have already developed sophisticated survival skills and cover-up tactics to cope with daily school life. Our task with them is threefold. We must:

    i. seek to undo the harm already done,
    ii. try to make sure it does not re-occur in those individuals,
    iii. learn to prevent any problems arising by putting together effective programmes right from the start.

Russell makes the very important point that 'All teachers, both classroom and physical education specialists, should be made more aware of the stages of physical development in children' (p.13). I should take this a stage further and advocate that this awareness be a compulsory part of infant and junior teacher training. *After all, if one thinks of the variables any teachers face, with regard to entering their new school — e.g., space, equipment, group size or time allotted to physical development — it is essential for them to understand the implications of what is available to them, so that they can construct motor development programmes which will suit their own children, their own school and their own individual way of working.* Delayed motor development and its prevention — and I cannot say this too often — is a matter for *all* teachers. Specialists are there as an aid and not as the answer.

Nevertheless it would be foolish to deny that every class teacher is in need of some kind of framework which will provide him or her with a basis for future work. But I stress that a framework is a framework, not a programme, and in consequence whatever guidelines are offered, whether in this book or elsewhere, should be seen as pointers not as prescriptions.

Each child has a place on the continuum of physical ability. The information you have been given thus far should enable you to identify where each of your children fits on such a continuum. I have deliberately left the scale open ended so that the definition of 'full potential' is not limited to the adult aspirations for such children. For

Figure 4.1 Continuum of Physical Ability

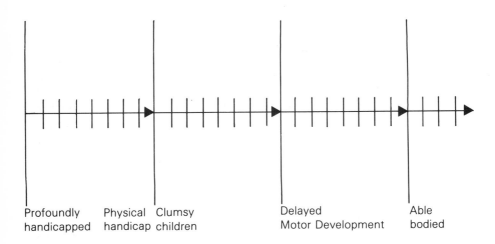

| Profoundly handicapped | Physical handicap | Clumsy children | Delayed Motor Development | Able bodied |

we must try not to impose upon them a restricted view of what their complete development should be. Physical, mental and psychological planes co-exist and correspond: each influences the others and is influenced by them. Therefore we must not assume that because a child has reached a stage in one of these areas, which we are happy to label 'good', he cannot go any further. Close the book and you end the story. Leave it open, and the story can go on. *Mens sana in corpore sano* is a goal, but not necessarily the end of the journey.

How to Develop a Curriculum

When you come to develop a curriculum, it is essential to remember that if any physical experience is to carry meaning for a child, he or she will need to experience it in very particular ways. I see these as four in number:

1. *Repetition* — It is fundamental to physical development that for an action to become an acquired skill, it must be repeated time and time again.
2. *Frequency* — In young children, especially those suffering

DMD, failure to repeat acquired skills frequently will result in a deterioration of those skills. Frequent use will make skills more readily applicable to day-to-day physical activity or competitive games and other sports.

3. *Variety* — All skills must be applied through a variety of situations in order to avoid boredom, maintain interest, and stimulate curiosity. We can clearly see a link here for the many games at our disposal and children's intrinsic desire to be competitive in a very innocent way. We must not be afraid to tap into this valuable resource, because it will enable children to make progress at a much greater rate. This leads me to:

4. The activity must make some kind of *Emotional Impact*. We have to make the adrenalin flow. This may happen through fear of the challenge ahead, through the intensity of the activity (yes, it must be hard work, too) or through the exhilaration of success, particularly in front of peers. More often that not it will be the straightforward feelings of fun and enjoyment, which only the individual concerned can quantify. As an adult, you can measure such impact only by the children's willingness and desire to repeat these experiences, and perhaps through their trust in allowing you to lead them into new and maybe more daunting experiences.

Let us bear in mind also that each individual session should attempt to allow the child to experience activities which will test and challenge the components of efficient motor function, i.e., the building blocks of sound motor development. Moreover, when you are working with 'clumsy' or DMD children, you may well wish to channel a given session in a particular direction, for example, balance activities or gross motor activities. But you must look at the time which is available to you and ensure that you apply the curriculum in a balanced way, not only through the school year, but also through every lesson — not as difficult a thing to do as it may appear.

A common notion I have encountered in this field of work has been that a relatively small amount of activity done more often is more productive than large chunks carried out infrequently. If we can bring about this state of affairs and adopt a spiral approach to applying the curriculum, i.e., one step backwards will help us to go two or maybe three steps forward, then we shall be in a very strong position both to prevent children from suffering delays in their motor development, and to remediate those who have already slipped through the net.

Let me now come to the method and attendant problems of developing a curriculum. Ideally one would like a timetable where each day would give the children some time to be spent on a physical activity, from the very first day of their school lives, using a range of activities which would satisfy developmentally the acquisition of the components of efficient motor function. Realistically, however, you will probably get a timetable which will allot two periods per week to physical education.

Figure 4.2 illustrates how physical education may appear on such a timetable[3]. But how does this fit in with the physical education experience that the child will pass through in school between the ages of 5 and 16? Nearly all schools maintain a compulsory element of

Figure 4.2 Junior School Timetable

		9.40–10.40	11.00–12.00	1.15–2.15	2.30–3.30
MONDAY					
TUESDAY	ASSEMBLY		Games— Winter Spring Swimming—Summer		
WEDNESDAY					
THURSDAY				Movement—Winter Spring Athletics —Summer Rounders	
FRIDAY					

physical education through this age range, and if we consider the implications of this, something like the picture given in Figure 4.3 emerges. The pressure created by this scheme of things has an effect on the programme offered in the junior school, which in turn has effects upon the physical education in the infant school. In other words, we expect children at a very early age to become competent quickly.

But what about those children who find all this difficult? One can see from Figure 4.3 how easy it is for them to be left behind. Where on earth is the additional time they need to live up to what will be expected of them physically? Perhaps the most frightening aspect of this picture is that it represents what they will have to cope with as an everyday part of their school life and makes no mention of clubs, teams, or competitions.

Figure 4.3 Chronological Flow of Physical Activity in the School Timetable

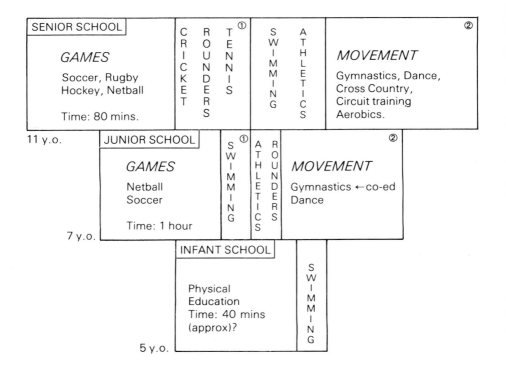

For the able-bodied of course, there are no apparent problems. But DMD children, who will begin to fail as early as the infant level, have an unenviable future of being given more time to spend on physical education, and in consequence, even more opportunities to fail. As long as this model continues to exist, all such children will be put in the situation of having to opt out, or having to develop techniques to avoid their failures becoming the focus of attention. Any hope of remediation, therefore, will be a decidedly hit and miss affair.

So how do you effectively start to offer this process within your own school? The answer to this quite simply is *time*, the most valuable commodity in any school. Teachers are reluctant to give up the time they have with children unless there are good reasons for doing so. Therefore the first step you must take in initiating any change in the school curriculum is to be absolutely sure why you think the proposed change is necessary. A sound knowledge of what you are talking about is essential to good practice and invaluable when it comes to bargaining with your colleagues for extra time. I hope, therefore, that your reading of this book so far will have provided you with at least some of that information you require.

The second step is to apply the knowledge you have to the situation which exists at the moment. As soon as it can be seen that your new approach is effective within the constraints of the existing timetable, the climate for adaptation and then (if necessary) wholesale change will become much more favourable, and your negotiations with colleagues will be much more fruitful as a result.

During this period of change you must be on the look out all the time for variety. Be critical of all the programmes in which you are involved and try to view them from the perspective of the components of efficient motor function and if the variety of programmes you offer, in the light of those components, leave clear 'gaps' in the children's development, then you must search for ways to fill those 'gaps'. Begin also to adopt the same critical standpoint towards the children you are teaching and very quickly you will begin to notice those with real problems, as well as those who excel. The former are the children for whom you will need to find even more time, so you must be very specific in identifying where they are weak.

In this short-term phase, any adjustments you make will undoubtedly start to produce improvements in the children's condition. These improvements will be significant in the sense that they will be visible not only to you but also to your colleagues. A child hitherto physically dormant, for example, will start to pick up and take an interest in his or her surroundings and in what is happening to him or her. Perhaps he or she will even begin to take an active part in the proceedings and, however small that part may be, it could represent a big change for the better as far as both he or she and you are concerned.

So now is the time to start the process of negotiation with other staff for more time for your children. First of all try to arrive at a consensus about what you are achieving with your current input, and then be specific about what you wish to achieve with the children in any additional time you can negotiate; and do remember that the concept of a 'relatively small amount of activity carried out often is more productive that large chunks done infrequently' is an important one for you to establish. Four short active sessions, for example, may well be more desirable than two long ones. But to get them, you will have to persuade Staff that the consequent alteration to the timetable is not the end of the world. Actually if you can get Staff to understand that this is, in fact, more productive than infrequency, your negotiations should proceed smoothly to the benefit of all concerned. If you look back at Figures 4.2 and 4.3 you can see quite clearly that time increases but not frequency. Room for manoeuvre in the senior tier is restricted by the subject-based timetable. (It has been possible to create time here and I shall come back to this in the section on school links, p. 104). The junior and infant schools with their class-based approach allow for more flexibility.

Now for the negotiation! First, do not present your request as a straightforward 'I want more time'. Look at the time you have already. For example the junior timetable in Figure 4.2 has two lessons of one hour, i.e., two hours per week. Is it possible to reshape this into three lessons of forty minutes each? The lessons, although shorter, will, with good planning and an increase in pace, certainly be as productive as two longer sessions, and may well be even more so. In order to fit in with the mechanics of the school day you may have to suggest as a start three lessons of thirty minutes each — an actual cut in time, but an increase in frequency, which is what you are aiming for. A third option may be to take two lessons for thirty minutes each and one lesson for an hour, which maintains frequency and does not lose time. This particular option may fit into the present school timetable more easily than others. Nevertheless, the onus is on you to do your homework. Look at the possibilities of increasing frequency in your school. Be sensitive to the requirements you are making of your colleagues and above all be seen to be flexible. But be in no doubt that what you are asking for is right, and you will find that once you have made the concept of frequency for all children acceptable to your colleagues, they will find it easier to accept the argument that these particular difficulties should, virtually as of right, be granted more time on the timetable. Let us now suppose you negotiated extra time — what do you do with it? The important thing to remember when you have gained additional time is that the activities which fill it must provide a balanced curriculum. Figures 4.4 and 4.5 illustrate how you can bring about the appropriate balance of activities with very young children and how you can develop that curriculum through to the senior age group.

Comments

1. These are actual curricula which have been developed along the lines I have described.

   With all children, the lesson will begin and end with core activities. But sooner or later you will want to branch out and use part of your new negotiated time for other activities. What happens here is that material from the core is fed into those additional activities — as much as you think is required by the individuals with whom you are currently working. Slowly, or not so slowly, as the case may be, the dominance of the core activities alone will diminish, with the result that the children's skills will be honed to increasingly greater levels of sophistication and in consequence can be used more and more in the wider curriculum. Notice too, that the curriculum is sufficiently flexible to cope with the needs of older DMD children

Figure 4.4 Infant – Junior Curriculum, 6 years old

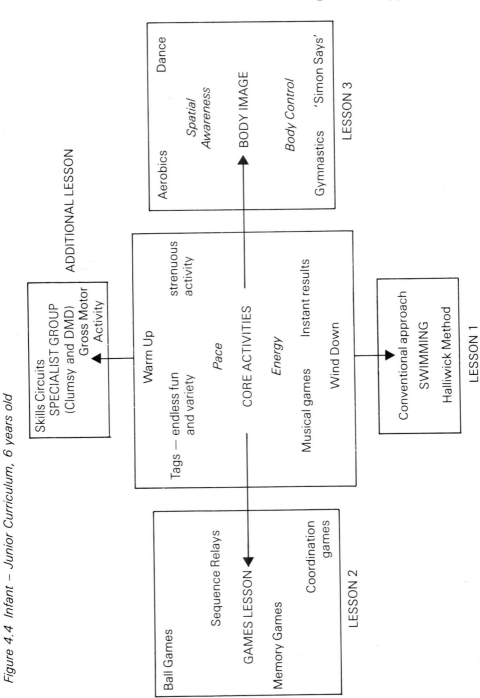

Figure 4.5 Senior Curriculum, 13–16 years old

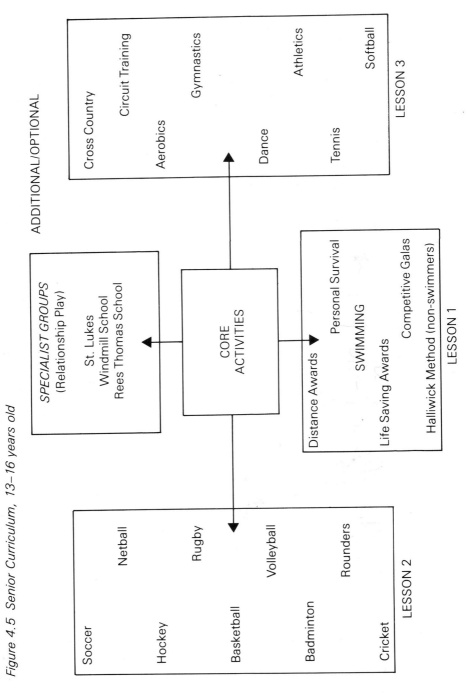

who can be helped by increasing the core activities in each lesson, or focusing upon body image, or spending more time on sequencing, etc.

The sooner the children's physical education starts along these lines the better, because we can then ensure that all children arrive at the senior curriculum (which mirrors the normal comprehensive curriculum with the addition of a safety net) less daunted, more skilful and more enthusiastic for exercise, because the emphasis has been on their ability not their inability.

2. Be careful to let everyone else on the staff know what you are doing and when you propose to do it, partly so that you can pool the skills and resources of the staff to the benefit of all, and partly so that you avoid activity clashes, for instance, physical education on the same day as folk dancing.

3. Developing such a curriculum does not happen overnight. The examples I have given took nearly three years to develop, so remember that patience is a virtue.

Indicidentally, let me make a point which I shall be making more than once as we go along. Children who are physically dormant need to be woken up. They find physical activity a real strain and it serves no useful purpose to allow them to avoid this part of their development. Colleagues who work alongside me with the physically handicapped as well as 'clumsy' and DMD children have become convinced, as I have, that these children can be lazy, moody and even stroppy when you apply pressure on them to work hard. You must not be afraid of applying or even intensifying such pressure. Don't accept the 'I can't' excuse because 'I can't' usually means 'I won't'. It may be stating the obvious but it must be said that we must not feel sorry for these children. What is required is in fact *non-sentimental* caring.

Specialist Groups: Why have them?

If you look at the content of the PE curriculum in a good many schools — I should actually say the majority — you can see straight away that most of what it offers is relevant to the needs of most children in the school and is often able to satisfy their apparent requirements. What such a curriculum does not do, however, is cope with the needs and demands of those children in the school who, for one reason or another, do not benefit from the experiences and activities on offer: and it is these children, of course, who most frequently enter the downward spiral of failure to achieve, loss of self-confidence and, in the end, loss of self-esteem, which in turn leads to more failure, more loss, and so on.

This was the growing impression I had when I looked at the PE programmes originally offered in my own school and it was the realization that something really ought to be done, and could be done, to ameliorate this situation, which led me first of all to seek the help of, and then to form a close liaison with, both the school physiotherapist and the local Child Development Centre.

Visits to the centre I found especially interesting. Each week, children diagnosed as 'clumsy' were brought there by their parents for two hours during school time, and the work which was done on developing the children's motor skills during these sessions was really first class. Here, it seemed to me, was an admirable solution to part of the problem: a full range of therapists working with first rate equipment in a purpose-built facility. But 'part of the problem' is the key phrase here. Only the most damaged children in the 'clumsy' category could be accommodated, and many of them were having to travel long distances and miss quite a lot of school time. By the Centre's terms of reference therefore, very few, if any, of the children from my school would have qualified to join this group, so the problem remained: what to do with the children suffering from delays in their motor development? The answer seemed obvious: create a group along similar lines in school. There will be certain immediate and certain long-term benefits, the most obvious being that the child can work in a group of similar ability on tasks designed to meet his or her specific needs with a guaranteed high level of success. As a group they are less likely to be stigmatized as something 'odd' or 'different'. No time is wasted on unnecessary travelling and it creates an opportunity for those invisible children, those with minor delays in motor development, to be fed into a programme until they are remediated. It is also a more effective way of supporting and supplementing any work the physiotherapist may wish to carry out with individuals. The long-term benefits are clear: the check and reversal of the downward spiral (i.e., success), increasing confidence and better self-esteem, subsequent enhancement of classroom performance and — an important point — a school running such a group ensures that any new child enountering real movement difficulties will have those problems addressed as a matter of right rather than by chance.

Three problems however, were apparent from the start — a. how to convince the staff of the need to release children from academic lessons, b. how to avoid stigmatizing the children, and c. how to find a slot on the timetable which would suit all the staff. Initially we justified the release of eight children on the grounds that they were already being treated as individuals by the physiotherapist. This input was to be curtailed, something which would, in this instance at any rate, do no harm and might even do some good, because some of the children were not responding well to individual withdrawal and individual specialist treatment. On the evidence of the group I saw at the Child Development Centre, I became convinced that the variety and emotional impact of any activity is greatly enhanced when children work in groups, and subsequent experience has reinforced this belief.

Possibly the most difficult concept for the classroom teacher to grasp is why the time for the 'clumsy' child is not taken from the existing PE allocation. The answer to this is stigma. Withdrawal makes these children 'different', and being 'different' creates a barrier between them and their peers. We have already looked at reasons which may have caused their problems and we have also identified the pattern of their PE as they progress through their schooling. One thing is certain — if they have some kind of label hung round their necks by their peers and maybe even by their teachers, removing them from the very area in which they need a boost and support will simply help to give even greater substance to that image and reinforce again their negative perceptions of themselves. The spiral must be reversed. An avenue to which they can turn must be created for them so that they can begin working at activities with which they feel comfortable, at tasks at which they can succeed, in a manner which attacks head-on their particular motor problems. For example, were a child to be a non-swimmer, you would not keep throwing him or her into the pool during the lesson. It is more likely that he or she would be encouraged to attend the non-swimmers' club to supplement his or her swimming lesson. Why not do the same with 'clumsy' children? The net result of all this will be a much more active, confident and able child who is willing to take on more difficult tasks in the regular PE session[4].

Initially, the only way to create a slot on the timetable was to use personal, non-contact time. However, such was the success of this group that during subsequent timetable discussions, the motor development group was amongst the first penned in, other activities and lessons being fitted around us!

Specialist Groups: How do we staff them?

How to staff such groups revolves around one simple question — who needs the power? Traditionally teachers have exercised complete control over both persons and events in their teaching situations, and I remember that I found it difficult to come to terms with the presence of other people in the room when I began to work in special education. In the main these 'other people' are welfare assistants, but volunteers, parents and older pupils (say in the 15–19 age group) may also come into lessons from time to time.

The traditional power of the teacher very often has the effect of reducing the extra help to a subordinate or 'monitorial' role. This is not to say that such a role has no place in the lesson or is not beneficial. Assistance in dressing and undressing the children, getting out and putting away apparatus, as well as relieving the teacher of small administrative chores, e.g., compiling, distributing, collecting lists, etc., is undoubtedly valuable in that it allows the teacher to concentrate on the business of teaching, thus maximizing the use of the teaching time available. The danger of such an approach is that it clearly demonstrates to the children who it is that is in charge and negates any possibility of these 'other people' being fully able to provide an adequate role-model for the children during the lesson.

They will not be perceived as teachers, with all that implies in the traditional situation, and so there is also a slight danger that they will not be taken as seriously as they should be, either by the children or the teacher him/herself. Psychological perception works both ways. How the teacher perceives his or her own role is likely to be the way he or she is perceived by others, and so an authoritative figure (however caring or understanding) cannot but impose that self-image on others as well as on him or herself.

Now, my own reservations about the traditional notion of teacher power are that in this type of group it is an inefficient teaching strategy. It must be remembered that these children are limited in their physical and learning capabilities. I would certainly feel more confident with a more teacher-centred strategy where the children concerned were not experiencing such difficulties. Making the teacher the focus of the lesson results in, a. much less 'hands on' attention, i.e., DMD children will often need physical manipulation through the early stages of learning a new skill, b. a reduction in the number of eyes for the purpose of observation and assessment, essential for the identification of the real problems facing the children, and c. lost opportunities for increased praise for individuals wherever success is achieved, which is vital if real progress is to be made in the area of self-esteem and confidence.

Certain obvious conclusions now present themselves. First, as far as special needs groups are concerned, it is not only highly desirable but even essential that people other than the teacher should be present. This will provide the children with alternative approaches, access to different skills and a wider range of learning experiences; and their presence will both provide new types of activity for the children and satisfy the earlier requirements of giving DMD children not only repetition and frequency of activity but also variety and emotional impact. Secondly, teachers will have to come to terms psychologically with the team-teaching strategy. Abdication of permanent sole control by the teacher within the lesson produces a fluid situation in which power is passed, rather like a medicine ball, from hand to hand. Those temporarily without the power actually benefit by having extra time to observe, assess, and deliver hands-on assistance where required and this, of course, can only be good for the children. Moreover, the children themselves are perfectly happy to work for anyone (irrespective of his/her status) who has good ideas and who delivers them with belief and confidence.

So, if we are agreed that others should and indeed must be involved, how do we go about making them feel as though they are an integral part of the teaching process? The answer is actually quite simple:

1. find out the hidden talents of members of your own staff,
2. find out the range of abilities and interests of the extra people,
3. let each side know what the other can do.

When it comes to putting this into practice, do remember that people are often reticent about their talents and so it is quite possible that you will not necessarily know how much your colleagues have to offer. So begin with the staffroom itself. Ask, cajole, wheedle, exercise charm! Find out what can be offered, and encourage as many as you can to join you in helping to open out the children's experience. After all, many if not most of your colleagues will have children of their own, and will be employing all kinds of strategies already with great success. Raw enthusiasm, of course, however laudable, is not quite what is required. Informed enthusiasm is what will do the job, and therefore a certain amount of training is desirable before you introduce expansion of the teaching element in DMD groups. Not every local authority provides the same amount or quality of such training, so you will do well to check your local situation first.

Earlier on, in my list of possible assistants, I mentioned older children. They have a distinctive role to play, and therefore should be included in any plans you make, if they are available. Energy and pace are the two most obvious qualities a 15- or 16-year-old can bring to a 7-year-old, who will react to these in a manner different from the way in which he or she would react to an adult. What is more, one-to-one relationships, so important for the development of DMD children, are much more possible if one has children working with children — and here the older child helps to stretch the younger one's abilities. He or she can be as strong as his or her partner — and also stronger; as lively — and livelier; as fast — and faster. But when the situation calls for it, he or she can let his or her strength go and allow the younger child to 'win'.

It sounds, does it not, rather like a parental role? But then, these older children are indeed the parents of the next generation and one of the benefits of such interactive lessons for them is that they are given an opportunity to learn what their natural parental instincts are, how to exhibit them without embarrassment or fear, and how to develop them. Notice, too, the implication of giving them such a role. We must release to them, for the time being, some of our authority as adults. The responsibility which they are now being asked to carry for someone else must be a real responsibility. What is more, the older children themselves must know this and be told so openly. The effect, as I have observed it on so many occasions, is to increase their confidence, their self-esteem, their caring qualities ('tenderness' would be an even better word), and these are passed on to their partners during the lesson. *Sympathy*, as the Greeks understood it, or *consentio* as the Romans might have expressed it, is thus developed between them.[5]

Check List of points

1. Decide to involve other people in your lessons.
2. Collect information and ideas.
3. Disseminate information and ideas: facilitate their exchange.
4. Let other people, including other children, have power and responsibility in your lessons, let them have the reins.

Specialist Groups — What activities can we use?

When it comes to PE lessons, there are many sources of activities available to the teacher, for example, major team games such as soccer, hockey, netball and traditional movement for groups and individuals via gymnastics and the creative elements of dance, and aspects of these undoubtedly have a place within the activity plan for

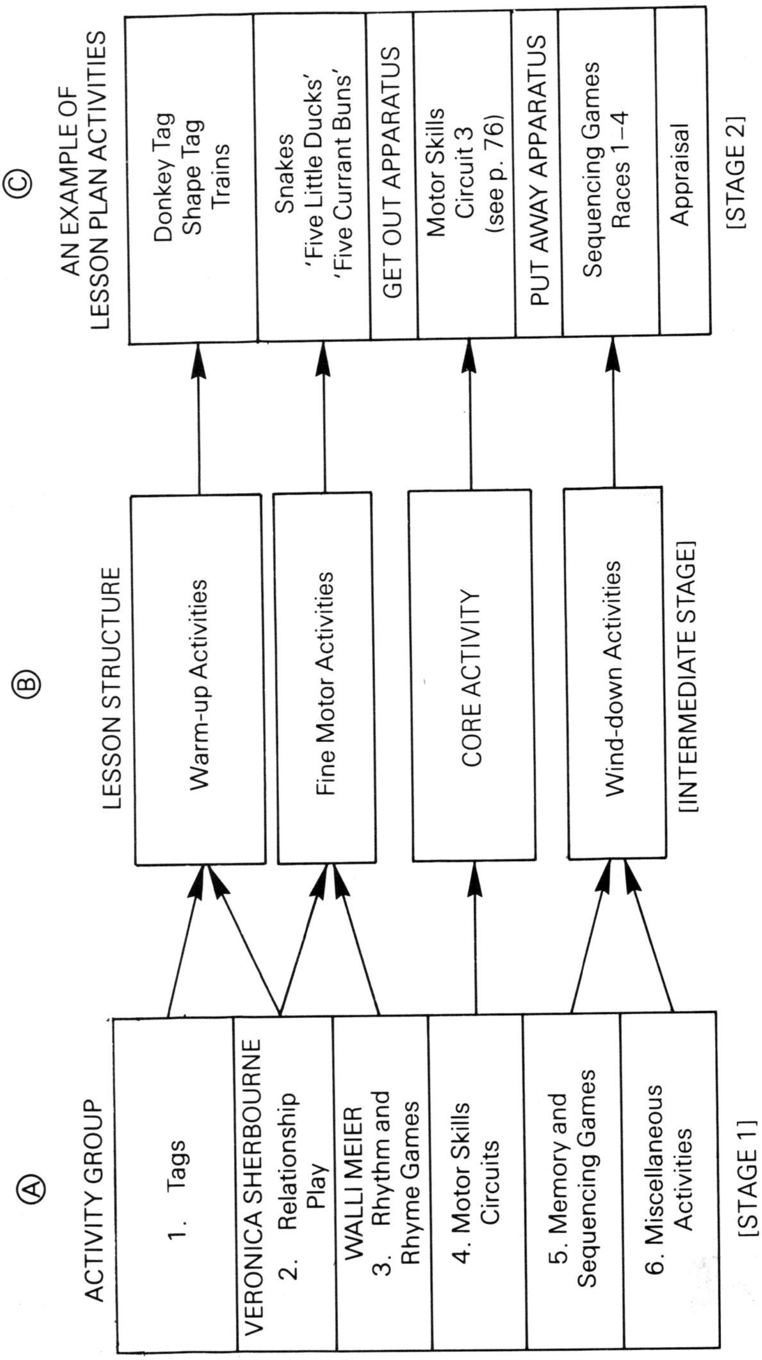

Figure 4.6 The Processes of Lesson Planning

Ⓐ ACTIVITY GROUP

1. Tags

VERONICA SHERBOURNE
2. Relationship Play

WALLI MEIER
3. Rhythm and Rhyme Games

4. Motor Skills Circuits

5. Memory and Sequencing Games

6. Miscellaneous Activities

[STAGE 1]

Ⓑ LESSON STRUCTURE

Warm-up Activities

Fine Motor Activities

CORE ACTIVITY

Wind-down Activities

[INTERMEDIATE STAGE]

Ⓒ AN EXAMPLE OF LESSON PLAN ACTIVITIES

Donkey Tag
Shape Tag
Trains

Snakes
'Five Little Ducks'
'Five Currant Buns'

GET OUT APPARATUS

Motor Skills
Circuit 3
(see p. 76)

PUT AWAY APPARATUS

Sequencing Games
Races 1–4

Appraisal

[STAGE 2]

specialist groups. One must remember, however, that the abilities which DMD children have been able to acquire will certainly exclude them from achieving excellence and without the support of activities which seek to cater for their specific needs, DMD children may well never be able to achieve even a low level of competence in these traditional areas.

It is for this reason that not only must we slot into our plan for their activity much of what we have learned from the physiotherapists, Veronica Sherbourne, Walli Meier and the Halliwick swimming method, but also that we must be looking to adopt and extract activities from the more traditional areas such as ball games, racquet games and athletics, so that we can devise lessons which give relevance to the work going on in the ordinary PE lesson.

The process of devising such lessons is what follows and can be described thus:

first, from all the activities which may be available to you, select those which form a natural and useful 'activity group',
secondly, from that activity group, devise a structure and pattern for the lesson with the objectives clearly defined.

This is your lesson plan. The intermediate stage, of course, is the process of deciding how you are going to make use of those activities you have chosen, and in consequence, the whole process can be best shown as follows: Activity Group — Intermediate Structure — Lesson Plan (see Figure 4.6).

Possible Components of Activity Groups

Group 1 — Tags

The combinations of these games are too numerous to mention in full, so I shall name specific games which you may or may not know and then deal more with how and why they operate in the way they do.

Having some type of ball with which to catch the children, initially by touching them with it, and then by throwing it at them is always popular. But it is vital that the adults have control of the catching first. This clarifies the rules and means that everyone and not just a few will get caught. When someone has been caught, he/she must pay a forfeit because this provides a way of getting him/her back into the game. The forfeits I myself favour support the development of gross motor strength, e.g., sit-ups, press-ups, bridging in various forms and squat thrusts. Always use one of the adults to help the child through this forfeit *quickly*. As long as they feel involved in the game, it is amazing how many forfeits they will fulfil. The quality of the forfeit improves with quantity in these games, not through coaching. This is, after all, meant to be a fun warm-up. Releasing each other can be equally hard work and should involve the children in crawling under bodies, jumping over bodies, copying shapes (mirroring), or simply being tagged back into the game by other children.

In the very early stages of a specialist group, these games are invaluable for improving the vitality of DMD children. Here, then, are six games of tag you might use over a period of four lessons.

1. *Stuck in the Mud*. When caught the child must stand with legs apart until another child crawls through his/her legs to release him/her.

2. *Ball Tag*. Catchers each have a sponge ball to throw. If caught, the child must do five sit-ups before rejoining the game. (You may wish to have some mats on the floor to make this more comfortable).

3. *Donkey Tag*. Each child has a band in his shorts or her skirt to act as a tail. The catchers each have one minute to collect as many tails as possible. Each child caught has to complete five press-ups. It is important to note that if you start this game, every child must get a chance to be 'it'.

4. *Chain Tag*. Start with two children holding hands. Each child who is caught joins the chain — an exhausting game this one — until there is only one child left. He or she can then pick the forfeit

for everyone else. (They usually pick one hundred press-ups, so you may have to use adult discretion!).

5. *Shape Tag*. Again, let each catcher have a ball. Throwing a rugby ball along the floor, for example, creates a whole new set of problems for those being chased, because of the unpredictable roll. Should the ball hit them, they must make some kind of shape with their body. When somebody else copies that shape, they can rejoin the game. You will find it necessary to demonstrate, or for certain children to demonstrate a variety of shapes, and of course you are able to condition the game with a specific shape.

6. *Welly Tag*. The children seemed to enjoy chasing each other in oversize wellies. I mention this to illustrate the possibility of using everyday objects to add to the fun.

As soon as possible delegate the catching power to the children because this frees the adults to home in on individual children who may need to be pulled around, be helped with the forfeit or simply sparked into life. The main problem with this group of activities, incidentally, is that it is easy to over-run one's time, they are so much fun.

Group 2 — Relationship Play

Before moving on to apparatus, the children can gain a lot from working one-to-one with another body (adult or child) and the Veronica Sherbourne techniques lend themselves readily to this section. They are particularly useful in focusing on the strength activities. Obviously I cannot describe here the whole range of Sherbourne activities and so I shall merely describe a few which might be used within the lesson plans.

1. *Back to Back*. Here the children sit back to back on the floor, feet and hands spread and on the command 'Go!' attempt to push each other backwards. It is a competitive and strong activity.

2. *Trains*. Adopt the same position as described above. Number

each other one or two. Take turns at pushing the partner, back to back, around the hall. Change over.

3. *Prisoners.* Number one sits between the legs of number two, who then wraps his/her arms and legs tightly around his/her partner. On the command 'Go!' number one must release him/herself from the prison. Change over.

4. *Starfish.* One lies face down on the floor and tries to stick to it. Two has to pull the starfish over on to its back. Change over.

5. *Parcels.* One curls up his/her body and wraps his/her arms around the back of his/her legs, pulling him/herself together as tightly as possible. Two attempts to unwrap the parcel and straighten it out. Change over.

6. *Snakes.* One lies on his/her back, head down to the ground and lets his/her body relax. Two then picks up one's legs at the ankles and pulls his/her partner's body along the floor, first sliding it, then trying to swing it gently from side to side as they move along, following a snake-like path. Change over.

There are many more combinations of the above relationship play, and you may well be aware of some already. The physical activity involved in pushing and pulling and squeezing someone else can provide a lot of hard work for one's whole body. Notice too, that there is a lot of scope for competition in these activities as well as cooperation and therefore there are good opportunities to improve self-esteem and confidence.

Group 3 — Rhythm and Rhyme

This group of activities will not only begin to focus the child's attention on specific body-parts and their relationship to other parts (body language), but will also reveal the range and variety of movement of which each body part is capable. In particular, we are hoping to improve on the fine motor skills.

The work of Walli Meier, who believes that all children need to develop an intimate knowledge of their body parts (body image), provides us with another group of activities which fits rather well into the overall scheme of things.

You might begin this section, then, by massaging or patting hands, feet, knees, elbows, making sure that the children not only look at that body part, but make significance of it. Here we can teach the children about falling and rolling, and so give them the confidence to look after themselves. It is also important for each child to identify him or herself to the other children. We must give them a chance to state their worth and feed into them a feeling of belonging and thus boost their confidence. Two excellent ways of achieving this involve sitting around in a circle and playing the name game. First, clap three times and on the fourth beat — silence; one, two, three — sssh!, one, two, three — sssh!. Now replace the 'sssh!' with one child shouting loudly his or her name. One, two, three, 'Jenny', one, two, three, 'James', etc. The whole group has to clap the — one, two, three, rhythm. This is a difficult task in itself, which may take a long time (with such children) to perfect. An alternative is to ask each child in the circle to roll backwards and then sit up again in a flowing movement. During this activity the child must call out 'My name is Tracey /Kevin /etc.,' each in turn. Again this provides a physically demanding exercise. These activities are excellent tools for introducing the new members into the group, a situation which arises frequently if other schools wish to use the group as a resource.

When the children are in a circle it provides an ideal setting to play the finger and arm nursery rhyme games. Once more these are numerous and those which follow are just a few examples with which you may be familiar.

(a) 'Incey wincey spider climbed the water spout...'
(b) 'This is the church and here's the steeple...'
(c) 'Five little ducks went swimming one day...'
(d) 'Five currant buns in a baker's shop...'
(e) 'The elephant walks like this and that...'
(f) 'I can tap with both feet, both feet, both feet...'

All these and many more can be found in such books as the *Springfields Song Book* (Springfields School, Huntingdon), *Bright*

Ideas — Games for PE (Wetton, 1987) and *This Little Puffin* (Matterson, 1969) and complement the work on body image rather well. Even children whom you may think too old for this type of activity, but are delayed in their motor development, find this a great deal of fun. Indeed it may well be that only now are they capable of succeeding at this type of activity, whereas at nursery school it may have been an area for failure.

Group 4 — Motor Skills Circuits

These circuits are, in fact, the core activity of the lesson, and while I was observing the 'clumsy' group at the Child Development Centre in Cambridge, it became obvious that of all the activities in which the children took part, the skills circuit would most readily transfer to the school PE lesson.

X X = children

Figure 4.7 Working in Straight Lines

The advantages of including such circuits are threefold. First, you can if you wish produce a circuit which will satisfy, in one part of the lesson, the majority of the components of efficient motor function. Secondly, you can bias the circuit towards the particular needs of individuals or group requirements, e.g., more balance activities or more gross muscle activities. Thirdly, the circuits can be constructed using the simplest of equipment, such as can be found in most schools.

One must not assume, however, that by placing a number of pieces of apparatus around the hall, interspersed with a few obstacles, the children will immediately make sense of it all. Remember many of these children are physically switched off and will therefore need the sequence of activities you wish them to follow to be built up little by little.

Figure 4.7 illustrates a good starting point for all children. The children move between the mats, one at a time, in a variety of ways, e.g., crawling, running, hopping, bunny-jumping, skipping, etc. You can increase the difficulty by giving them something to hold, dribble or even balance on the head. It can, if you like, be a competitive race.

Let us now move on to stage two, shown in Figure 4.8. At this stage we have introduced two obstacles: a series of hoops for them to jump into, and a cane on skittles for them to crawl under. Again, you can add variety and increase difficulty as the children succeed.

And now stage three, shown in Figure 4.9.

Finally, we introduce some simple apparatus and give the children a new direction in which to travel. The children now work their own way around the circuit, one at a time, from each mat, and finish when they return to the original mat.

It is important for the children to go through these seemingly simple stages in order to establish a basic pattern for working their way around the more complex circuits (examples of which are given in Figures 4.10 – 4.15) and you may find that at times the children will need to be carried physically through the moments of confusion. By making the children go through these stages, you will clearly identify those who have severe problems with regard to space and direction, and sequencing, and of course this means you can bias the obstacles and apparatus in favour of specific motor functions so that all these areas can be brought under scrutiny.

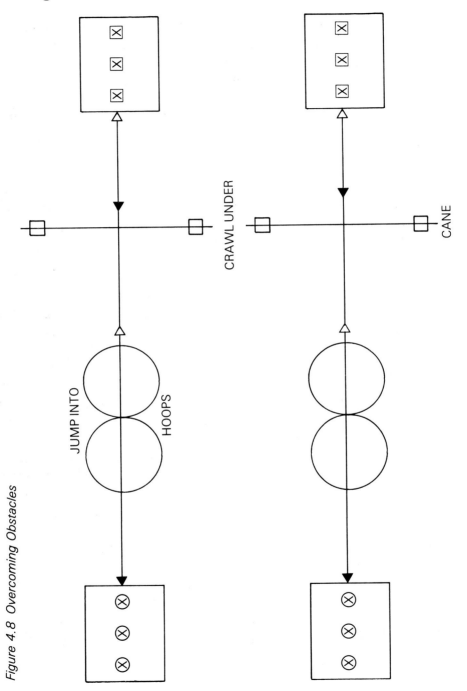

Figure 4.8 Overcoming Obstacles

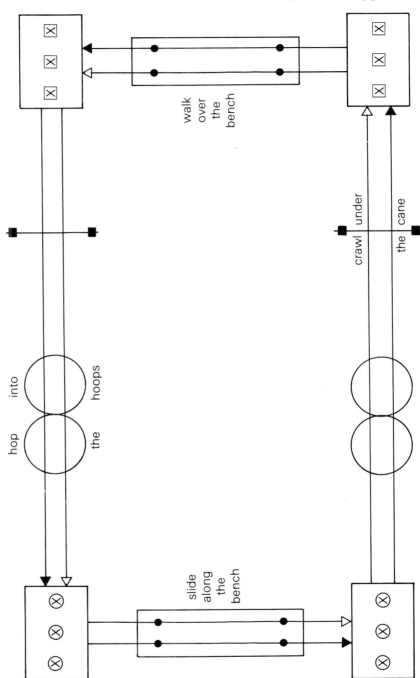

Figure 4.9 Introduction of Circuiting Obstacles and Apparatus

Figure 4.10 Skills Circuit 1

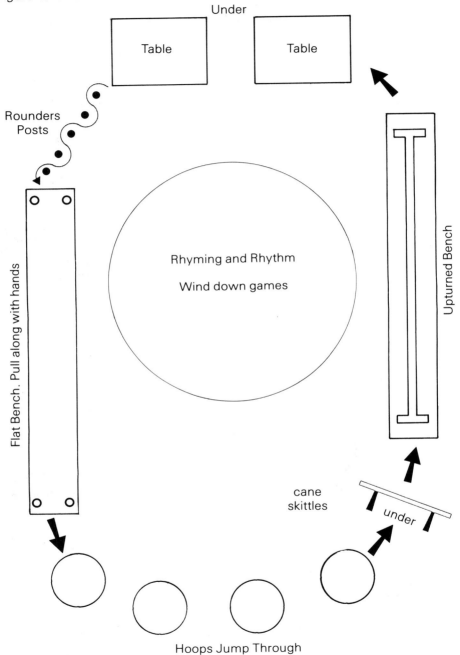

Figure 4.11 Skills Circuit 2

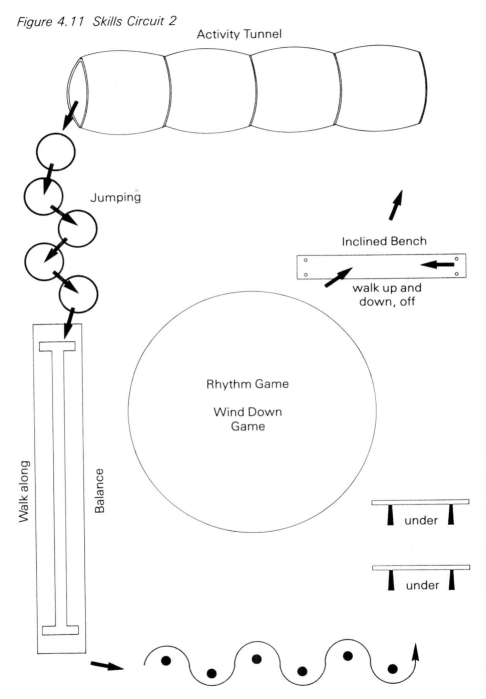

Activity Tunnel

Jumping

Inclined Bench

walk up and
down, off

Rhythm Game

Wind Down
Game

Walk along

Balance

under

under

Figure 4.12 Skills Circuit 3

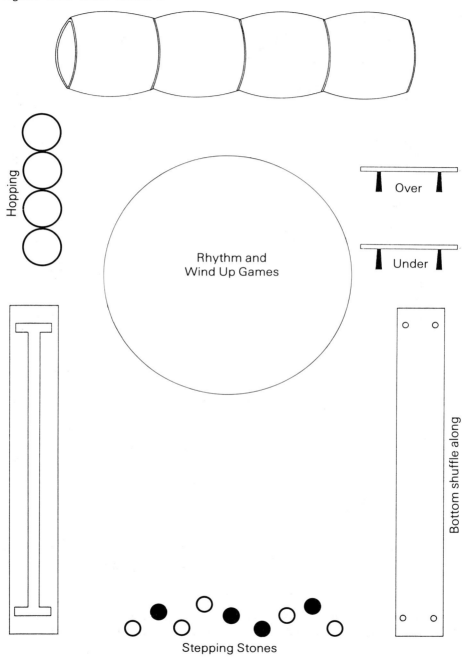

Figure 4.13 Skills Circuit 4

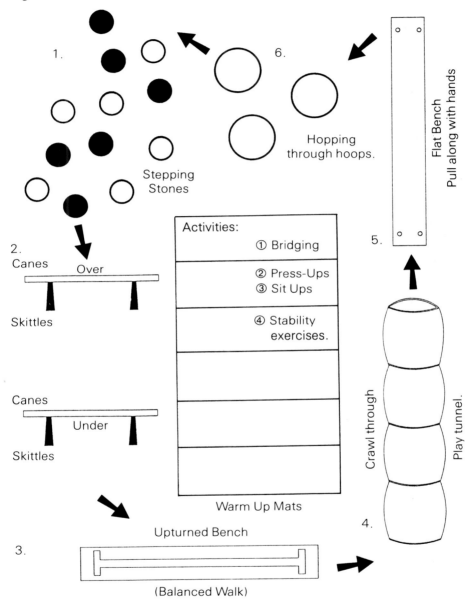

Wind down games include: varieties of tag, Memory games i.e., Duck, Duck, Grey Duck. N.B. Children to take responsibility for putting apparatus away.

Figure 4.14 Skills Circuit 5

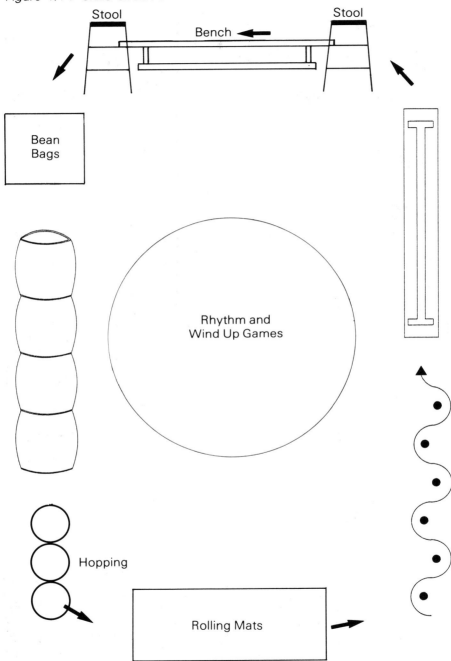

Figure 4.15 Skills Circuit 6

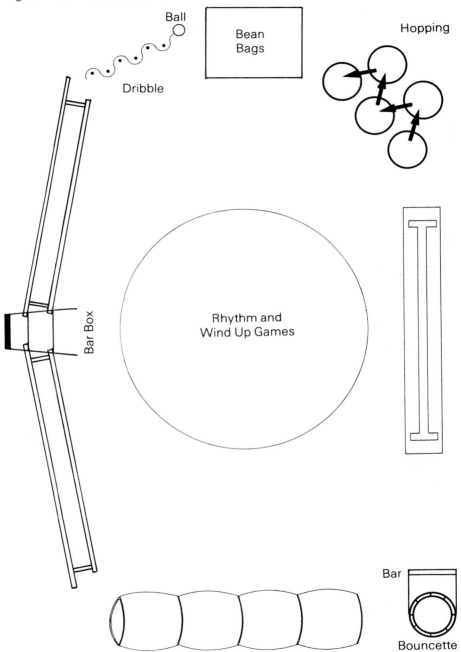

How long should each of these circuits last? I recommend that, in theory at least, they should be repeated over a four week period. If the children progress quickly and achieve a fair measure of success, the elements of any circuit should be changed, or made more difficult by, for example, altering height, distance, elevation, or width of surfaces and apparatus. It is also advisable to organize the children in apparatus groups and to maintain those groups throughout the active life of the circuit. They can be allocated to specific pieces of apparatus which you know they can handle safely.[6] Notice that you also have incorporated into the lesson a memory test:

Who is in my group?
Who is the adult leader?
What apparatus am I responsible for?

Group 5 — Memory and Sequencing Activities

In this type of activity, children are requested to memorize situations and follow instructions which increase in complexity. You can incorporate these activities into team situations or as individual play within a set game. Here are two examples which I have used with great success.

1. *Sequencing Games.* Divide the group into four teams (remember that small team numbers offer more activity for each individual) and give each team a gym mat as its base. Set up a skittle or rounders post opposite each team at the other end of the hall. The object is for each player to make his/her way from base, round the post, and back again until the whole team has taken part.

Race 1: Run round the skittle and back to the mat. The signal for the next person to go is to be touched on the head by the incoming runner.

Race 2: Hop to the skittle and run back to the mat. Change over as for race 1.

Race 3: Hop to the skittle on your right foot and back on your left foot.

Race 4: Run to the skittle, complete five sit ups, and hop back.

As you can see, you can develop this group of activities in many ways, e.g., adding equipment for the children to carry, varying the exercise, changing the mode of locomotion, or using the feet to dribble balls, etc. It is important that each time a new instruction is added, the children clearly hear what is required. Adult support will become essential for many children as complexity increases. I always endeavour to end at a point where every child has independently completed the same sequence of activities.

2. *Memory Games*. An excellent example of such a game is 'Duck, Duck, Grey Duck'. The children sit round in a fairly close circle and one child is nominated to stand and move out of the circle, leaving a space. He/she must make his/her way around the outside of the circle, touching each child upon the head. As the contact is made, she/he must shout out 'Duck!'. At any time he/she can change the call to 'Grey Duck!'. The person who has been nominated 'Grey Duck' has to rise and race him/her back to 'Grey Duck's' place — not the original space — and the first person back to the open space sits in it, whilst the person who comes second continues the game, circling in the same direction. In the early stages of playing this game, the children will often fight for the wrong space. The game can increase in complexity in two ways: i. Having two people circling at the same time, but in opposite directions. The children then have four spaces to memorize as well as the direction. ii. Silent 'Grey Duck'. In this game, instead of shouting 'Duck' or 'Grey Duck', the children must tap the head once for 'Duck' and twice for 'Grey Duck'. The rest of the game proceeds as for i., or the original game.

Sequencing and memory games lend themselves readily to adding a competitive element to the lesson, as well as contributing the expected variety and fun. Other games which can be played here are 'Simon Says', 'Hot Potato' and the 'Newspaper Game'.

Group 6 — Miscellaneous Activities

By now I hope you will have begun to visualize how the many activities, games and exercises that you know will fit into the 'specialist group' jigsaw. I must stress that the ideas given here do not and are not meant to afford 'The Definitive Specialist Group Programme'. It is entirely up to you to vary, invent, reconstruct, according to the children you have, the space and equipment that are available, and the inspiration of the moment. Don't forget music. Well known standard games such as musical chairs, 'The Grand Old Duke of York', musical statues, are obvious starting points. But passing fads from TV films, discotheques — anything with a beat, rhythm, a simple (or fairly complex) range of movement — will suit your purpose equally well.

My point is that in order to avoid the possibility of your being taken over by the structure and therefore having your creativity stifled, be prepared to throw in activities which keep the structure alive, and to make this task easier, do consult your colleagues who could well have a multitude of ideas stored inside their heads.

Lesson Structure

Having gathered your activities together into useful groups, you need to produce a structure into which they will easily flow. In any lesson of physical activity it is essential that the children be given an activity which quickly gets under way, requires very little dialogue and provides a certain amount of fun. With specialist groups, however, you must home in with activities in ways which affect specific motor skills. Therefore any warm-up must ensure that both gross and fine motor activities are included. Activity groups 1, 2 and 3 above lend themselves readily to this.

The core activity of our lesson — the motor skills circuit — is where all the hard work is done, and to which the bulk of the available time must be devoted, because while it is going on, you have to make sure you tackle, at least in some measure, all the components of efficient motor function.

After winding down, the children must leave the lesson with a feeling that they have participated fully in what was going on, that they have achieved at least a modicum of success, and that it was important for them to have been there and to have taken part. This is how they grow in confidence and self-esteem, and so it is vital that the wind-down activities, examples of which are to be found within the activity groups 5 and 6, be within the capabilities of all children, no matter how simple those activities may appear to you.

Lesson Plans

The intermediate stage, lesson structure, provides the basis upon which you hang the activities in varying combinations, the net result being the *Lesson Plan*. The test of whether or not it is a good plan will be whether it satisfies our main requirements, i.e., do the children encounter all the components of efficient motor function which are listed below:

1. Symmetrical Activity
2. Basic Body Movement
3. Gross Muscle Development
4. Fine Muscle Development
5. Eye-hand Coordination
6. Eye-foot Coordination
7. Body Image
8. Balance
9. Rhythm
10. Space and Direction.

What follows in Figures 4.16 – 4.19 is a group of lesson plans which are designed around motor skills circuit 1 (see Figure 4.10) and are meant to run for a four-week period. The final column indicates which motor functions are being exercised at any given time in the lesson. Notice that if you have planned your lesson correctly, all the components should be affected in one way or another and with varying degrees of frequency throughout the course of the lesson.

Figure 4.16 Lesson Plan Week 1. Time – 1 hour

LESSON STRUCTURE	ACTIVITIES	COMPONENTS AFFECTED
WARM UP ACTIVITIES	'Chain Tag' 'Stuck in the Mud' 'Back to Back'	1, 2, 3, 5, 8 and 10
FINE MOTOR ACTIVITIES	'Starfish' 'Name Game' (clapping) 'Incey Wincey Spider'	1, 3, 4, 5 and 9
	GET OUT APPARATUS	
CORE ACTIVITY	MOTOR SKILLS CIRCUIT (1) (see Figure 4.10)	1, 2, 3, 4, 6, 7, 8 and 10
	PUT AWAY APPARATUS	
WIND DOWN ACTIVITIES	'Duck, Duck, Grey Duck' Roll out of the gym	2, 3, 5, 7 and 10
APPRAISAL		

Figure 4.17 *Lesson Plan Week 2. Time – 1 hour*

LESSON STRUCTURE	ACTIVITIES	COMPONENTS AFFECTED
WARM UP ACTIVITIES	'Stuck in the Mud' 'Ball Tag' 'Trains'	1, 2, 3, 5, 8 and 10
FINE MOTOR ACTIVITIES	Parcels 'Incey Wincey Spider' 'Name Game' (rolling)	1, 3, 4, 5 and 9
	GET OUT APPARATUS	
CORE ACTIVITY	MOTOR SKILLS CIRCUIT (1) (see Figure 4.10)	1, 2, 3, 4, 6, 7, 8 and 10
	PUT AWAY APPARATUS	
WIND DOWN ACTIVITIES	'Simon Says' Slide out of gym on your back	1, 2, 3, 7, 8 and 10
APPRAISAL		

Figure 4.18 Lesson Plan Week 3. Time – 1 hour

LESSON STRUCTURE	ACTIVITIES	COMPONENTS AFFECTED
WARM UP ACTIVITIES	Ball Tag Shape Tag Snakes	1, 2, 3, 5, 7, 8 and 10
FINE MOTOR ACTIVITIES	Prisoners 'Five little Ducks' 'This is the church'	3, 4, 5 and 9
	GET OUT APPARATUS	
CORE ACTIVITY	MOTOR SKILLS CIRCUIT (1) (see Figure 4.10)	1, 2, 3, 4, 6, 7, 8 and 10
	PUT AWAY APPARATUS	
WIND DOWN ACTIVITIES	Musical Statues Swim out of the gym on your front	3, 7, 8 and 10
APPRAISAL		

Figure 4.19 Lesson Plan Week 4. Time – 1 hour

LESSON STRUCTURE	ACTIVITIES	COMPONENTS AFFECTED
WARM UP ACTIVITIES	Shape Tag Chain Tag Back to Back	1, 2, 3, 5, 7, 8 and 10
FINE MOTOR ACTIVITIES	Starfish 'This is the church' 'Five Currant Buns'	1, 3, 4, 5 and 9
	GET OUT APPARATUS	
CORE ACTIVITY	MOTOR SKILLS CIRCUIT (1) (see Figure 4.10)	1, 2, 3, 4, 6, 7, 8 and 10
	PUT AWAY APPARATUS	
WIND DOWN ACTIVITIES	Hot Potato Bunny Hop out of the gym	3, 5, 8 and 10
APPRAISAL		

This type of structure has two clear advantages for children in specialist groups. First, it provides them with opportunities to work continually at groups of motor skills, and this avoids the problem of their dwelling upon specific weaknesses for any length of time — an important point, because they are thus given more chances to succeed through the use of those abilities they actually have. Secondly, the structure provides plenty of occasion for *repetition* and *frequency* of activity and these, in turn, automatically give the lesson scope for variety. So those children who have hitherto suffered from a depressed profile of skills will now find themselves moving on an upward spiral of improved ability, improved confidence and enhanced self-esteem, and once this has started to happen, you will know that you have fulfilled the fourth requirement of the exercise, *making an emotional impact.*

Specialist Groups — How long should the children stay in such groups?

There is, in fact, no simple answer to this question. Let me illustrate this with four examples of children who have recently left my DMD group.

1. Christine was among the original eight children who formed the first DMD group in school. Having been scored at a very poor sub-5-year-old level on the Test of Motor Impairment (TOMI) as a 7-year-old, she was an obvious candidate for the group. Two years later, she is now capable of functioning with the ability 'norms' of her peer group. Maintaining her presence in the group would have begun to renew the stigmas that I had fought so hard to remove.

2. Julie has medical problems which will always cause her to stand out physically from the norm. However, after eighteen months with the group, natural growth and an increase in age mean that she no longer fits easily into it and I have therefore transferred her extra PE session to my adolescent DMD group. Her confidence and self-esteem, however, are at an all-time high.

3. Derek joined the school at 10 years old and had particular problems with balance and spatial orientation. He was, in fact, very

timid physically in spite of his large physical presence. He could have left the group after two terms but his obvious enjoyment therewith and feeling of achievement made me decide to keep him for another term, after which he left.

4. James joined us from a local junior school specifically so that we could tackle what were called his 'motor problems', although relative to the children in my school, these so called problems were minor. In consequence it was not long before James found himself in the position of being very able physically in comparison with the other children in the group. It was interesting to note, as the weeks progressed, the positive change in attitude to any task that was presented to him. He rejoined his own school after two terms with us.

Now, what are the obvious points to be drawn from this? I can see two. First, the children should stay in their group for as long as it takes to bring them within the norms of their peers. There will of course be problems associated with this. For example, how they develop physically may set them apart from others in the group, or medical difficulties may place obstacles in the way of their achieving the desired goal. To overcome both types of problem, I created a different type of specialist group higher up the school, especially for such children, with the aim of providing them with extra opportunities to close the physical gap which separates them from their peers. Continuing to work with children obviously younger than themselves would almost certainly run the risk of their becoming re-stigmatized as 'clumsy' or 'disabled', and that is something we are trying very hard to prevent.

Second, there are two very good clues which let you know that these children ought to leave the group. Their abilities will begin to exceed the challenges put before them, and the lesson will then begin to lose its emotional impact and the children's behaviour patterns will start to change. For example, you may start to notice increasingly boisterous behaviour or increasing signs of boredom. Also, and this I find is the most important sign, there is a major shift in the children's psychological reaction to your command or request. I have already drawn attention to the initial interactions in such situations: 'Do this'. 'I can't'. 'Yes, you can and you *must!*'

Sooner or later, there will come a point when you give a command/make your request, and the child will carry out the task automatically, without stopping to think 'Can I?'. Somewhere along the line, during your remediation treatment, that block has been removed, or at any rate significantly shifted, and when you see that that has happened, you will know it is time for that child to move out and move on. However, do not forget that the notion that they stay 'as long as it takes' must be underpinned by the *certainty* that when you withdraw this support, their normal PE allocation will satisfy their physical developmental requirements. On a purely practical front too, make sure that, a. you consult the class teacher regarding an appropriate moment to re-integrate the child back to the classroom, and b. you let the other children in the group know why one of their members is leaving. It is because he or she has been successful and his/her success can be theirs if they continue to work hard, work well, and seek a similar goal. This 'signing off' process underlines the notion of achievability for everyone, and therefore helps to reinforce the positive aspects of everything you are trying to do.

Concluding Remarks

I should like you to finish reading this chapter with three distinct impressions formed in your mind: first, DMD children do exist; secondly, they need support; and thirdly, it is perfectly possible to provide them with all the support they need. But I must also ask a question. Do you really have a desire to tackle the problem, knowing the various obstacles which may stand in your way? It is essential that you do, because my experience is that the type of group I have been describing can do an awful lot of good for a very large number of children in terms not only of their physical development, but also their all-round maturation. My aim, and I hope yours too, is to make these children feel the joy and freedom of movement by helping them to unlock their bodies. For when a child truly feels good about him or herself physically, the avenues to learning also rapidly open before him or her.

These following photographs illustrate two different types of specialist groups described in Chapter 4. Photographs 9–12 show DMD children at work; photographs 13–16 illustrate profoundly handicapped children in various relationship plays with mainstream adolescents.

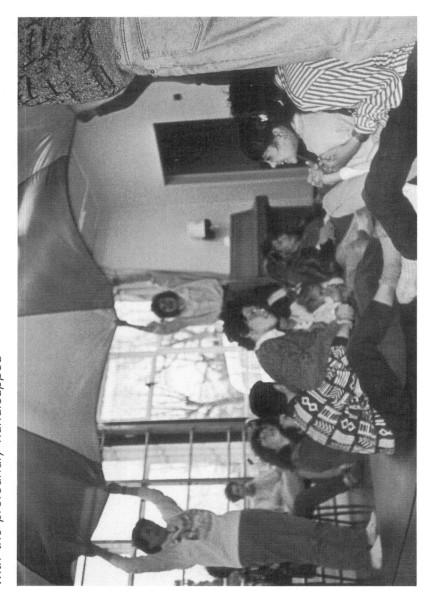

Illustrations 4.9 and 4.10: Fourth year mainstream pupils enjoying parachute games with the profoundly handicapped

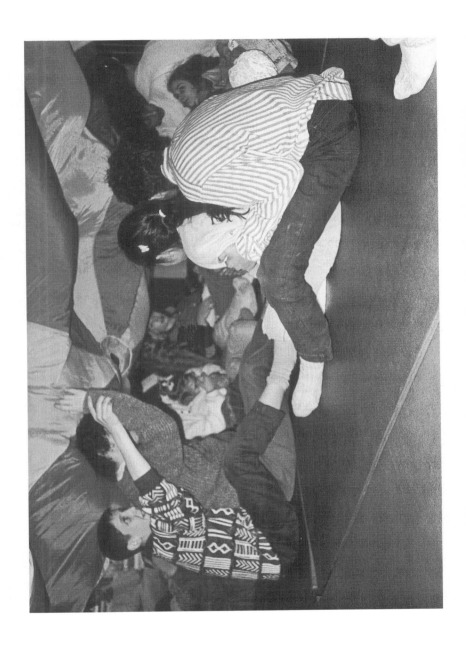

Illustration 4.11: Working with partners

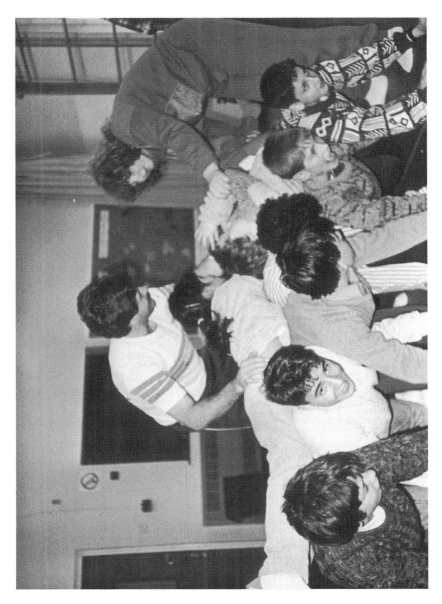

Illustration 4.12: Working in groups

Illustration 4.13: 'Five Currant Buns' — Developing fine motor skills

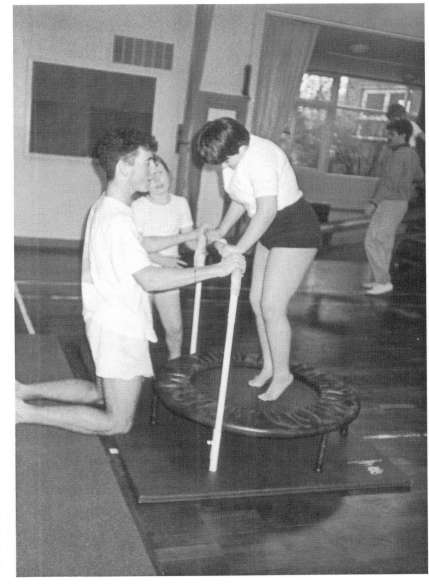

Illustration 4.14: Sixth form student helping DMD children on apparatus

Illustration 4.15: 'Walking the Plank'

Illustration 4.16: 'The light at the end of the tunnel!'

Notes

1. For example, Russell says that when a child is having problems with reading and writing, we should refer him to the educational psychologist so that the reasons may be diagnosed [p.11]; and again when a child is thought to have motor difficulties, Russell recommends that he be sent to the school's medical officer and the educational psychologist who will then give their opinions on what is causing the motor difficulty [p.12]. Thus 'Non specialist teachers (in physical education terms) need prescriptive programmes to which they can refer' is Russell's conclusion. This raises important questions: a. What is the role of the physiotherapist? b. At what point should the non-specialist be asked to make a real effort to understand what the problem is and what the child's difficulties actually are? c. How often is the non-specialist supposed to waive personal responsibility and personal involvement in favour of 'letting an expert take the strain'?
2. Everyone will agree that the treatment of such children, as individuals or in small groups, may stigmatize them within their peer groups. Are we in danger of classifying the children into academic and non-academic, and should we not be looking at children with such difficulties purely in motor developmental terms? (Russell, incidentally, comes near to contradicting himself when he divides delayed motor development children into academic and non-academic [p.10], but then adds the cautionary word that 'it is all too easy to label children' [p.12].
3. Where a school has a specialist facility, for example a swimming pool or a teacher who has a particular expertise such as country/folk dancing, it may choose to make use of them in addition to its normal physical education programme. But these are not the norm and therefore it is still a matter of chance, rather than a matter of right as to whether a child will find such opportunities on its timetable.
4. It is interesting to note how quickly colleagues notice the benefits of this approach for such children. The increase in awareness, the improvement of concentration span, the reduction in fidgeting, the willingness to listen and interpret instructions more readily, observed in the original eight children, has produced a constant flow of candidates for this group. It seems that when children learn to come to terms with their own bodies they become far better recipients of learning.
5. It is worth noting too, that these periods of responsibility will quickly and naturally alter any misconception the older children may have about their role and relationship with the younger. He/she is not indulging in a pseudo-charitable enterprise — 'I the healthy, am doing

good to the handicapped' — but is meeting another individual on the level of caring difference.

6. As with any other group, time will have to be given to the safe handling of equipment and the mechanics of lifting. This must be re-enforced continually.

Chapter 5

Establishing Links

Linking Across Phases and Schools — A Case Study

We have now reached the stage where I think it will be useful to cast an eye over a real case history, that is to say, a review of a particular attempt to create groups both within a single school and then across a series of local schools. So what follows is a résumé of my own experience during the past two and a half years, and is meant to illustrate the successes and warn of the pitfalls which can happen during the course of such an endeavour.

First Phase (Autumn 1986 — Summer 1987)

Establishing the Sherbourne Group

My attention was first alerted in Autumn 1985, by having children withdrawn from my PE lessons so that they could work with a physiotherapist and this led me to see if I could identify the special physical needs of the children within the school. This investigation in turn made me feel that it was very important to create opportunities for support in PE right across the school population. (In the case of Lady Adrian School, this means 6–16-year-olds).

The first specialist group (summer 1986) was aimed at the DMD children in the 6–11 age range, vertically streamed, and based its activities on the kind of lesson structure and lesson plan covered in Chapter 4. I then formed a second specialist group consisting of adolescent Lady Adrian children (MLD, 13–15-year-olds) who were linked with children from the nearby Rees Thomas School (SLD, similar ages), meeting once a week for a period of 45 minutes. This became known as the 'Sherbourne Group' because of the type of activities upon which its work was based.

What I found here was that the SLD children benefited from the experience while my own MLD children simply remained static. I wanted them to develop to the point where they could begin to take charge of their SLD partners in one-to-one relationships, but this was not happening because the MLDs were not yet physically or psychologically secure enough to be able to take on that role. They were still at the recipient stage themselves and did not know how to cope with the process of giving. As a result, I ended up teaching the whole class according to the traditional, teacher-dominant role, and this was not what I wanted.

The thing which broke the stalemate and enabled us to make real progress was the introduction into the group of 15-year-old children from Chesterton Community College. These adolescents were sufficiently sure of themselves physically, at least in relation to the whole Sherbourne group, to be able to adopt the relationship-play I was looking for, and in consequence they provided the catalyst which was needed. From this point onwards, progress among both the MLD and SLD children was marked, and participation in relationship-play began to have a beneficial effect on the Chesterton pupils as well.

So far, two terms had passed. It was now Easter 1987, and many of these Fifth Year children left school. I therefore sought Fourth Years from the same school to replace them, and at the same time introduced a group of non-examination Fourth Years to work with a group of 6–8-year-olds during the summer term. This group consisted of DMD children as well as children without any physical problems.

Taking Stock

With three specialist groups operating by the end of summer term 1987, coincidentally the end of the academic year, it seemed an appropriate time to take stock of what had happened so far, in order to see what form future development might take. The DMD group had proved itself to be highly successful and colleagues were quick to spot the benefits for the children by giving them this extra time. So when the group was given an established slot in the timetable, this had the full backing of the classroom teachers who were now beginning to suggest possible candidates for the group. For my part, I was continually on the lookout for ways to develop the curriculum content, and many of the activities covered in earlier chapters were added to the curriculum during this period of development. This DMD group is now a permanent fixture in the timetable.

Initial difficulties with the Sherbourne Group had been resolved by the addition of Chesterton pupils, but expansion of the use of such pupils in the junior–infant tier of the school created some new problems. Those of you familiar with the complexities of timetabling in a large school will understand the problem of asking for children to be removed from the timetable for short spells, such as one term. Since all lessons are proprietorially regarded as invaluable and therefore not to be missed, one might expect to be asked how any could be curtailed or switched or dropped in favour of 'extra PE lessons'. Special schools, by their very nature, are usually more willing to adapt their timetables than mainstream schools. In this case however, the problem was solved by having an initial group drawn from those children deemed to have special academic needs within Chesterton Community College and who were already working with a flexible timetable in special groups and so familiar with the process of being withdrawn from ordinary lessons.

Cautious of the situation I had created with the Sherbourne Group for my own MLD pupils, I was determined not to end up by simply adding more children to the group for *me* to teach, but to add to the group children who would be capable of assisting in the teaching process themselves. So I contacted the relevant teacher and we decided that it would be constructive to talk to the Chesterton group first about the nature of DMD and then give them details about those children with whom they would be working — their names, the schools they came from, their individual disabilities, what we hoped to achieve with them during lessons, and why we were anxious to involve them with the DMD children. The whole notion of educating the more able children in each group, in advance, about the issue of DMD proved to be vitally important in the development of all groups. Where this is not done very different results obtain! Notice a lesson here: if you are going to use older children as teachers of younger children, you must be prepared to take them into your confidence and to be seen to be doing so. After all, for a while they will be your colleagues — minor colleagues to be sure, but colleagues nevertheless — and so they should be and must be accorded the openness and respect which that status carries with it. There are no problems associated with this. Children will respond with requisite maturity.

As I have already said, the initial Fifth Year group left at Easter, but both Chesterton and I felt that the positive benefits of having adolescents work with DMD children of any age warranted our trying to maintain the link during the summer term. As there were now no Fifth Years available, we decided to attempt the same exercise with two Fourth Year groups, one from English and one from Science. Both had large numbers of children who at that time were likely not to be taking examinations at the end of the Fifth Year. This meant that negotiating them out of their regular timetable would not be too arduous a task. By the end of summer 1987 my experience of the two groups had reinforced my belief that such children benefit greatly from working with less able children.

Their semi-parental role — one which many may be fulfilling already inside their own families — seems to alert their instincts to the evolving needs of their partners, and this 'antenna'd response' takes the authoritarian out of a simple teacher–pupil relationship such as the one sustained, inevitably, by an adult, and relocates it in genuine affinity with their partners. It is an observed and observable fact that as the older children grow in confidence and self-esteem, the less able children also seem to blossom both physically and psychologically.

Although I had been working with this type of group for a relatively short time — one academic year is not really that long, although sometimes it feels like a century — I would have felt almost negligent had I not attempted to cement those links with other

The Right to Movement

schools, which I had already formed, and to create further links elsewhere in the local community. Development of such links during the rest of 1987 and 1988 took place very rapidly, and is shown in Figures 5.1 and 5.2.

Figure 5.1 Chronological Development of Inter-school Links

Autumn 1985	Spring 1986	Summer 1986
[Research]	[Research]	DMD Group (6–11)

Autumn 1986	Spring 1987	Summer 1987
DMD Group Sherbourne Group — Lady Adrian Pupils & Rees Thomas SLD. School (both 12–15 y.o.) & Windmill School (14 y.o.)	DMD Group Sherbourne Group — Lady Adrian & Rees Thomas & Chesterton C.C. 5th years & Windmill School	DMD Group Sherbourne Group — Lady Adrian & Rees Thomas & Chesterton C.C. 4th years Relationship Play — Lady Adrian (6–8 y.o.) & Chesterton C.C. 4th years.

Autumn 1987	Spring 1988	Summer 1988
DMD Group — & Arbury Junior School.	DMD Group — Lady Adrian & Arbury J.S. & Mayfield J.S.	DMD Group — Lady Adrian & Arbury & Mayfield
Sherbourne Group — Lady Adrian & Rees Thomas & St Lukes Infants/Juniors (5–9 y.o.) & Manor C.C. (4th year)	Sherbourne Group — Lady Adrian & Rees Thomas & St Lukes & Manor C.C.	Sherbourne Group — Lady Adrian & Rees Thomas & St Lukes & Manor C.C.
Dance Link — Lady Adrian School (6–9 y.o.) & Netherhall School 5th years.	Halliwick Group — Lady Adrian (10–12 y.o.) & Chesterton 5th year	Halliwck Group — Lady Adrian & Chesterton C.C.
	Windmill Group — Lady Adrian (14–16 y.o) & Windmill School (14–18 y.o.)	INSET Group — Lady Adrian (14–16 y.o) & Kings Hedges Nursery /Infants (4–7 y.o.).
		Leisure Group — Lady Adrian & Rees Thomas (Seniors).

106

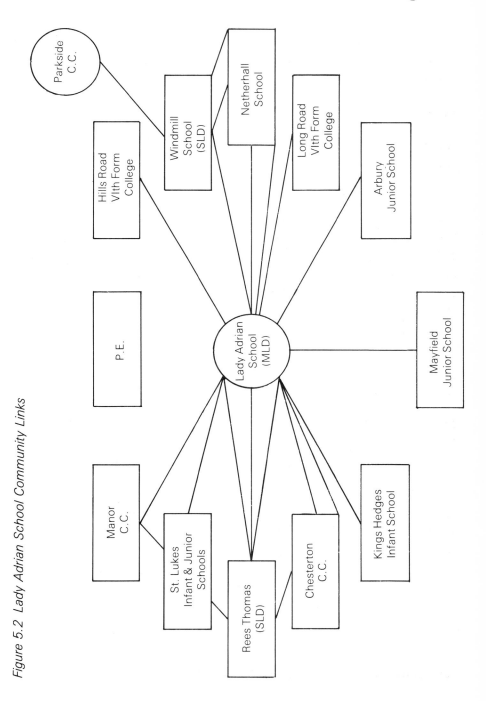

Figure 5.2 Lady Adrian School Community Links

Second Phase (Autumn 1987)

Things Go Wrong

The first phase of the Sherbourne Group had been successful and I was keen to press forward with the business of extending it into the community. This would have two results, or so I hoped. First, the new-found confidence and self-esteem of the Lady Adrian children could be developed further; second, other less advantaged children could be brought into contact with what proved to be a beneficial process. What I wanted to find was an infant/junior school which would be receptive to this suggestion.

It was my own headteacher who put me in touch with a school which appeared to answer my requirements. St. Luke's is a local C. of E. school which has both infant and junior age groups in the same building on the same site. The headteacher there was interested in the type of innovation I had in mind and St. Luke's had just had a brand new sports hall built. This I found a particular attraction because I assumed, quite mistakenly as it turned out, that such a hall would provide the ideal space in which to work my Sherbourne Group.

The first step was to meet the St. Luke's head, David Underwood, and discuss with him the philosophy of the group, and its proposed structure and modus operandi. I thought this went well. Our discussion was illustrated by photographs of last year's group and a video of a single working session. I took care to emphasise that a significant gap existed between the DMD children whose problems were essentially physical and those whose difficulties were rooted in emotional retardation (which of course expressed itself in highly physical terms). In other words, there could be two potential problems, one of movement, the other of behaviour.

Herein lay an unfortunate mistake on my part. By drawing such explicit attention to the potential problems associated with behavioural difficulties, I had unwittingly suggested that the new Sherbourne Group could make inroads into this area — perhaps even offer a cure — whereas what I should have done was to concentrate everyone's mind on the problems of movement, since these were the difficulties with which the group was designed and intended to deal. Misunderstanding over this point will store up trouble for the future.

For the moment however, all proceeded smoothly. The regular Tuesday morning slot was to continue, and for a group which now consisted of children from three schools — Lady Adrian, Rees Thomas and St. Luke's — four adults were provided; myself as leader, a teacher from Rees Thomas, a welfare assistant and a volunteer. Thus the group seemed to fulfil all the criteria I considered important for the successful operation of such a group:

several adults	— we had four
plenty of space	— we had the new sports hall
two groups of children appropriately matched for relationship play etc.	— we had sixteen adolescent and sixteen junior/infant DMD children
a regular slot in the school timetable	— we had 45 minutes each Tuesday morning
an additional PE lesson for all the children	

Despite all this, I began to feel uneasy almost as soon as we began. The reason was perfectly clear: the activity was ill-matched with the children we had, and this basic maladjustment was made worse by other factors. Perhaps the easiest way for me to explain what went wrong, and how, is to relate my comments to some of the criteria I have just mentioned.

The new sports hall for example: I had always thought that my own school's hall provided a particularly awkward working space — too small, open to traffic between school office, lavatories, canteen and the playground — and so a purpose-built facility twice the size and completely free from disruption seemed to be ideal. Four problems, however, reared their ugly heads in the very first session and they are well worth my drawing to your attention.

1. *Acoustics.* Frankly, the place was an acoustic nightmare. The materials used and the curved design of the roof amplified sound and echo alarmingly. The noise of the lesson became almost intolerable, especially for the younger children, which was most unfortunate since one of the things I was trying to encourage was a sense of personal freedom to make noise. Now this is an important point: DMD children, because they are physically inhibited, may also suffer inhibitions about expressing themselves verbally, one might almost say 'clamorously'. In addition, all children spend a large part of every day in the classroom heavily restricted in the amount of noise they can make. 'Stop talking!' must be the command most frequently issued by a teacher. So, relax restrictions upon noise and you help to loosen the bonds of inhibition; loosen these and you assist DMD children to express themselves physically. If they feel they can shout — and noise is part of having fun, in itself a relaxing process — they may feel they can move as well. Freedom in one area encourages freedom in another. But the noise must be pleasurable; once it reaches the level where the children dislike it, they will begin to feel oppressed by it, and thus the potentially good use of noise is undone and nullified. The sports hall, then, was far too noisy and there was nothing we were able to do about it.

2. *The Floor.* It is a cardinal rule, all too often forgotten, that the floor upon which your group is going to work should be warm and comfortable. Children, especially those already suffering from disabilities, are less willing to put up with discomfort from the working surface than able-bodied adults who, in any case, have the bulk of their attention directed elsewhere. The floor in the sports hall was a hard, very cold, grain wood floor, not at all suitable for sitting or lying down or general relaxation. I should have noticed that right from the start.

3. *Space.* Plenty of space for the activities you have in mind is indeed desirable, but you can have too much of a good thing and the St. Luke's hall actually provided too much room. Whatever space you use should not only be large enough to give you elbow room, but also be sufficiently contained to provide a feeling of intimacy. Relationship play cannot work properly if the children find they have room to hide from each other. So the balance of spaciousness and

cosiness is one which you need to gauge carefully in choosing the facility within which most of your work will take place. Big, in this case, is undoubtedly not beautiful. In defence of my original enthusiasm for the hall, I should say that our group consisted of 32 children and 4 adults, and so the notion of having plenty of space seemed attractive at the time. Atmosphere, however, as events revealed to me, is more important than space.

4. *Shelves and Doors.* The sports hall had storage cupboards running the length of each of its sides, thereby creating a shelf which the children found almost irresistible. Climbing up there enabled those who wanted to opt out or play silly beggars to do so with irritating ease. In addition, two lightweight doors leading from the hall provided another opportunity for the opters-out to flounce off and flounce back with minimum of effort on their part (but maximum noise and disturbance) and so make their emotional point as publicly as possible.

These then, are examples of what was wrong with the physical environment. Unfortunately, there were one or two other problems as well. For a start, I overestimated the amount of advance the older children had made. By the end of the previous term I had formed the impression that the Lady Adrian and Rees Thomas pupils were beginning to develop self-esteem and self-confidence to a point where they could readily take on a semi-independent role with younger children, and to a certain extent of course, this was true. But summer had intervened, regression had taken place, and the break revealed the basic dependency which still, in actual fact, underlay their earlier confidence. It was not that no progress had been made at all, simply that the legs were still weak, the feet unsure, the steps faltering and uncertain. My house was not built on sand, but the rising walls were still fragile. Had we run the original 1987–88 group by itself for another term and then introduced it into St. Luke's, many of the subsequent problems might not have happened, or at least have been considerably reduced. Still, trying to make them run before they could walk was not the only problem. Another was the composition of the group from St. Luke's, with which I was asking them to interact.

Mainstream schools, through no particular fault of their own, tend to make up their minds about what constitutes a DMD child, using quite different perceptions from my own or those of a physiotherapist. They are liable to see 'incapability': can't write, can't sit still, can't concentrate, can't tie shoe laces, can't play football, can't vault, climb or catch a ball, in purely physical terms and so designate any child who falls into this general category as suffering from DMD. In fact, as I have mentioned earlier, problems which are actually behavioural are often confused with motor difficulties because emotional disability usually expresses itself in physical ways. Therefore, in setting up a DMD group, it is important to make sure you have genuine DMD and not pseudo-DMD children.

In mainstream schools, it is the physiotherapist who helps teachers to distinguish correctly, and her work and procedure I have described in an earlier chapter. My mistake at St. Luke's was to ask ordinary members of staff to select for me those children whom they considered should form part of the group; in other words, I asked them to take on the role of a trained physiotherapist, and in consequence the children who were recommended to me were a mixture of genuine and pseudo-DMD cases. So I ended up with a group in which a sizeable nucleus was capable of running rings — physically, verbally and intellectually — round those older children whom I was asking to take on the role of partner, assistant and mentor. Little wonder then, that the Lady Adrian and Rees Thomas children suffered a severe jolt to their confidence and self esteem.

A gloomy picture, then, but not one entirely without relief. Problems connected with the hall itself were intractable, but others could be resolved without any difficulty. A session of 45 minutes, for example, actually proved to be too long because the children from St. Luke's, to whom all this was pretty new, found a lesson of that length too protracted a time span for them to be able to maintain their concentration. All we had to do to solve that little problem was to shorten the session by ten minutes and voila! an optimum length of lesson was achieved. (Now that the children have had a year to adjust to the demands made on them, it is interesting to note that we regularly tend to overrun our time. Re-adjustment to a 45 minute session would now therefore be feasible).

The really important positive feature of the whole exercise, however, was the way in which the staff associated with the group coped with all the difficulties. Their quite extraordinary patience and thoughtful understanding over a long period of time made all the difference to very awkward circumstances and ultimately made the group a success. Without them the exercise might easily have failed.

Finally, I mentioned earlier that an extra PE lesson is necessary for children who belong to such a group as this. Each of the schools involved has provided extra time, I am glad to say, and the beneficial effect of this upon the children can be gauged perhaps from the fact that although the group has now been running for four terms, no one has suggested that the extra time is an administrative inconvenience, nor has anyone thought of withdrawing from the liaison with other schools. Success in the teeth of many problems is, it seems, still success. Nevertheless, I called this section 'Things Go Wrong' because that was the basic situation we were facing in the early stages of setting up the liaison with St. Luke's. We had thirty-two children with no apparent desire to form relationships of any kind, let alone one-to-one closeness, and also, within those thirty-two, a core of children who seemed almost to resent being with us at all. They did not know why they had been selected to form part of the group and manifested their resentment (or perhaps just bewilderment) by trying to break up every attempt at order or structure, and making as much noise as they possibly could.

Putting Things Right

The answers to the problems of the group, as opposed to the problems of the venue, were pretty obvious: the children needed plenty of work to use up their energy, the rules of the work had to be easy to understand and, above all, the work itself had to be designed to produce instant success. Once we had got everyone feeling confident that he or she could tackle the activities, and once we had seeded the notion that those activities, by their very pace and variety, were fun to do, then we could start to build again the kind of developing challenge which would bring the children on and do them some real good. What we used were games and gross motor skills with plenty of varieties of 'Tag'. Indeed the latter formed a large part of our initial lessons, with adults acting as chasers, then the older children, and finally the younger children. This gradually brought them from a situation where they were being worked as individuals to the point where they could start to work together as pairs, and at this point it began to be possible for us to make real use of Veronica Sherbourne's relationship play.

Thus we brought everyone through several stages, from an inchoate assembly of individuals who happened to find themselves together under one noisy roof, to a group with an accepted, acceptable identity. It took nearly half a term for this to happen, half a term during which the younger children found themselves working in competition with older and vice versa, growing in confidence as one-to-one relationships began to emerge of their own accord. Sooner or later, of course, this natural bonding needed to be made official, so to speak, partly so that it could be seen to have the administrative stamp of approval, partly so that those who had not yet formed a bond should be given one, since we had to make sure that no one was left out (or felt he/she was being left out) and partly to give coherence to the overall structure of the group. This was not a smooth process. Absences from school, whether on the part of the children or members of staff, made it difficult to produce the continuously operative structure I should have liked. Indeed, it proved too much of a problem and so now we rely almost entirely on the natural bonding process to form this structure for us.

So much then, for the first problem. What about discipline? In order to create an harmonious working situation, behavioural problems had to be dealt with at once, not aggressively but firmly, so that right from the start no one should be allowed to conceive the idea that hostile disruption could stop the flow of group work and group enjoyment. This is more easily said than done of course, but this is how we worked out how to proceed:

1. We decided that no one should be allowed to leave the hall and that there would be no shelf-climbing. These were not laid down as rules *ex cathedra magistri*, but anyone who attempted to opt out found him/herself being eased back

into activity, and before long the children worked out the rules for themselves.

2. Anyone who tried to leave the activity found an adult talking quietly to them or, if necessary, taking hold of them and *putting* them back into the group. (Do not be afraid, and I have said this before, of taking hold of children and physically imposing your will. If it is done non-aggressively there is no harm at all in it, and indeed, this may actually be the most appropriate way of handling a given situation. Notice those two words *non-aggressively* and *appropriate*).

It is important not to let individuals opt out. Above all, try not to exclude them. Exclusion may be exactly what they are seeking. Do not allow 'negotiations' to go on for too long. The child may have opted out in order to get the exclusive attention of an adult and this is unfair to the others. In addition, make sure that every adult present plays the negotiator at some point, so that no one becomes identified with that role, otherwise the authoritarian figure will be seen as dominant and the group will cease to be a group and become rather more of a pack.

Programme-structure and meeting the problems of discipline, then, went hand in hand. As a more harmonious atmosphere developed, nuisances found it less and less desirable to opt out, and as less opting out took place we were able to introduce more and more variety into our activities and so increase the attraction of staying within the group. Eventually we were able to produce half-an-hour's worth of good constructive, varied, enjoyable work within an ordered, non-oppressive structure, of which the following might be considered a typical example:

Everyone was required to listen attentively as the rules of each activity were explained. The business of listening was a specific requirement, and the children were to be left in no doubt about this. The activity would not begin unless they listened first.

Equipment was to be kept as simple as possible and its use was designed for sharing. Thus, balls of various sizes, hoops, skipping ropes, mats, an elastic rope, etc., could be used for activities such as ball tag, tug-of-war, towing, etc. (see further Chapter 4, pp.74–9)

The gym mats became the bases for many activities, as they were infinitely more comfortable than the floor.

After each activity, everyone returned to sit quietly in the centre of the hall. This calmed down the children and helped to make them more receptive to the next set of instructions.

All the children were given some sort of power through the activities. For example, during a tag, the child who is doing the chasing feels that he/she is in control of the activity, and this feeling of personal control is essential to increase self-esteem and self-confidence, both of which I have stressed again and again as aims of what we are doing.

The children were also assigned tasks to perform which involved their being sub-divided into smaller groups. One group, drawn into a whispered confabulation, planned an activity which it would carry out at the expense of another group, for example, taking prisoners, starfish, trains, etc. (see further Chapter 4, pp.67–8). This reinforces the notions of power and control I have just mentioned, but this time the individual is submerged in the group, as it is the group and not he/she who has the power. Cooperation with two or three others to achieve the goal therefore becomes important, and so 'sharing power' is the object of these particular exercises. Naturally, every sub-group must have a chance to play this dominant role during the session.

This guide to structure (useful hints might be a better way of putting it) implies careful initial planning and I cannot stress too strongly how important it is for you to know exactly what your aims and objectives for each lesson are, and to organise yourself, your helpers and your equipment accordingly. I shall return to this point again at the end of the chapter.

It had taken a whole term to get the group going properly, but when we held an appraisal meeting with the staff of St. Luke's, we were all delighted to be able to come to the conclusion that the group had been a success. The children now wanted to remain in the group, there had been noticeable beneficial effects upon their physical performance and concentration, and some welcome short-term effects on their behaviour too. Maintaining the group, we were told, would give these benefits a good chance of turning into permanent advances in the welfare and development of the children. Thus it was decided that the group should continue until at least the end of the academic year. I was delighted. A project which had hit so many snags right from the start had come through its period of jeopardy with flying colours.

Before going into a brief survey of the Third Stage of this development however, I think I should mention another link that was set up during that same Autumn term.

Netherhall Dance Link

In addition to everything else, this clearly illustrated that Fifth-Year children are very capable when asked to work with infant/junior children, and positively enthuse when given the chance to do so. I felt sure that not only DMD but *all* children in my school would derive tremendous benefit from experiencing interaction of this kind and therefore I started to look for ways to create links which would not be exclusive.

An opportunity to do this surfaced, as it were, under my nose, for it so happened that a 'Dance Animateur', newly appointed by the city council, was not only working with a performing arts group in the senior school at Lady Adrian, but also with some Fifth-Year girls at Netherhall, an 11–18 comprehensive in Cambridge. Now these girls were becoming interested in the actual process of teaching dance and had expressed a wish to see if they could instruct as well as be instructed. Here was my chance to form the broader links which I wanted, and so I was more than happy to arrange for a group of Lady Adrian children to act as their guinea pigs. A convenient time was arranged — 45 minutes once a week, which was actually the normal PE session in our infant–junior school — and the whole group was staffed by one adult and the Fifth-Year Netherhall girls. Three adults from Lady Adrian were present, but assisted only when asked to do so.

The children were taken through a range of movement activities and games, and worked on a piece of dance-drama based on the story of Noah's Ark, a tale which was also being used in Lady Adrian as stimulus material for their classroom work. 'Noah's Ark' was then performed as a set piece at the end of term, with much success.

Although this was a one-off link which had come together fortuitously, it had important consequences. Another school had been pulled into the network of growing community links and the changes in social perceptions which flowed from this are worth further comment later.

Third Phase (Spring–Summer 1988)

Additions to the DMD Group

I was interested to note that 'Special Needs' PE, at this time, was beginning to attract national interest. More articles in the periodical *Special Needs* were being written about this aspect of children's education and the *Times Educational Supplement* also carried several articles on the subject. This raising of awareness, coupled with the enthusiasm of the local physiotherapists for the type of work we were carrying out, led to requests from other schools for their children to have access to this group. So during Autumn 1987 and Spring 1988 we began to take children from the Mayfield Junior School and Arbury Junior School. It looked as though Lady Adrian was starting to be seen as a resource for other educational establishments, fulfilling certain needs which they themselves were not in a position to meet.

Initially I was a little apprehensive about how these junior school children would handle the business of being brought to a special school for their PE, but I need not have worried. Once the children began to realize that these link-lessons enabled them to make all kinds of progress and that no-one was any different from anyone else, all hestitation on their part disappeared and the lessons were taken for granted. This acceptance by the children, and ensuring that no child in your school suffers as a result of links made with other schools, are vital.

The Windmill Group

Spring 1988 brought Lady Adrian into contact with a new and most significant group — profoundly handicapped children from the other local SLD school, the 'Windmill School'. We had had one boy from this school before, Kevin, who joined the Sherbourne Group in Autumn 1987, but now Lady Adrian was being approached to form a link with children at the far (disabled) end of the continuum of physical development. It was to be a challenge of course, but one immensely worth meeting, since any advance we could make or help to make, would be that touch more important for the profoundly handicapped children concerned.

The fact that it was two special schools involved meant that individual timetables were more adaptable and Lady Adrian was able to select those children we felt would benefit most from the experience, boys and girls who were not necessarily DMD, but had poor self-images and negative feelings of worth.

The initial group was quite small, four from each school, and we chose to meet every Wednesday morning for 45 minutes in a classroom belonging to another secondary school, the Manor Community College, largely because the Lady Adrian children involved were already going there that morning for another activity. The space, however, proved quite inadequate and eventually we began to go across to the Windmill School where the group met with greater success. We employed techniques such as I have described earlier and although it was hard work, progress on both sides was apparent, and by the end of term everyone felt pleased by the relationships which the link had forged.

The Halliwick Group

In Autumn 1987 I had attended a course organized by the Association of Swimming Therapy on the elementary techniques of the Halliwick Swimming Method. Although this course was aimed at the physically disabled swimmer, it did seem to have many elements which were applicable to all non-swimmers, either able bodied, DMD or physically handicapped, the most obvious being the use of one-to-one human contact. I decided it would be a good idea to find a way of introducing non-swimmers in the middle tier of Lady Adrian to the benefits of this method.

There were, however, two problems. Lady Adrian does not have its own swimming pool and so our children use the pool in Chesterton Community College, the school I have mentioned already as an important link in setting up the Sherbourne Group. Could we get any Chesterton children off their set timetable and also give them enough pre-instruction to make them feel confident in dealing with the pupils from Lady Adrian? Pre-instruction actually caused no difficulty. A few teaching sessions done during several lunch hours solved that one and, as it happened, the set timetable problem almost solved itself. Our swimming lessons coincided with various Chesterton Fifth Year activities — PE and Community Studies — and the projected swimming link came at a time when disaffected Fifth Years were beginning to turn restless and uncooperative in the classroom. Eight of these, some of whom had already worked with us in the Sherbourne Group, eagerly took up the offer of doing something which they perceived as interesting, useful and enjoyable, and so the Halliwick Group got under way with minimal hesitation. Easter leavers and examinations had an effect during the summer term, but there were always enough children left to work one-to-one with the non-swimmers, and many of these who replaced the early leavers turned out to be just as keen to help as their predecessors.

The Kings Hedges INSET Group

Creating these various links in the local community stirred quite a lot of interest in what we were doing, and I was asked by the staff of Kings Hedges Infants School in Cambridge to provide them with a day's course on DMD children. It seemed to me, as a result of the day's experience, that the best way to capitalize on the new enthusiasm was to start another group, another link, and so we began a ten-week liaison between a group of Lady Adrian senior children and three separate groups of Kings Hedges infants in a good mix of boys and girls.

It was an interesting situation which, in certain ways, was not quite like anything we had done before. The seniors, for example, were accustomed to sessions lasting for only 45 minutes. Here they were required to work for 75 minutes, because the three Kings Hedges groups followed each other in three sessions of 25 minutes each — ample for children aged 4–5 years (Group A), 5–6 (Group B), and 6–7 (Group C). Being required to work with more than one group in an afternoon was also a novelty for the Lady Adrian pupils.

The very young children were initially somewhat intimidated by the older Lady Adrian children, as one might expect, and preferred to begin with 'Tags' and motor skills work rather than plunge straight into relationship play. After a while, though, apprehension disappeared and we were able to get them working on a full range of activities without any difficulty, a development which owed much to the endless patience and enthusiasm of the Lady Adrian children who took to their teaching, supportive role at once and sustained it throughout the whole of the ten-week period. These Lady Adrian children had no motor development problems of their own, an important factor in this situation, since, from the start, they were confident of their ability to do as they were asked. One might also note that the 6–7 year old Kings Hedges' children displayed no nervousness of relationship play, and thoroughly enjoyed the opportunity of coming into contact with other bodies.

Since Summer 1988, I have had the experience of working with a group of children aged 2½–4 years. None of them had any difficulty in coping with the core activities (see Figure 4.4) and although this was just a single session, I take it as an encouraging sign that their response was immediate and uncomplicated.

The Leisure Group

Although special schools are designed to meet a certain range of specific needs, there seem to be areas of overlap between them and this means that one ought to be able to move children whose abilities/disabilities fall somewhere inside those areas from one institution to another without causing undue stress or difficulty.

Bearing this in mind, I decided to create yet another link by setting up a group consisting of certain children from Lady Adrian (an MLD school) and Rees Thomas (an SLD school). The aim of this group was not therapy but pleasure and its activities included such things as carpet bowls, aerobics, table tennis, snooker and skittles. Staff from both schools supervised and after a while the group took on a club atmosphere. Careful matching of the children was important of course. They had to be of similar age, the intellectual and physical disability gaps had to be narrow, and they had to be compatible in terms of emotional maturity. This group has been very successful and many of the children now link in other areas of the school curriculum, too.

Summary

What can be said then, by way of general comment at the end of this three year experiment? Well first, and perhaps most important: it is no longer an experiment. Most of the groups I have described are still in existence and still operating successfully (the Netherhall Dance Link and the Kings Hedges INSET Group however were specifically set up as 'one term only' projects). Three major developments since Summer 1988 have been, i. that every pupil in the Third, Fourth and Fifth years at Lady Adrian is now given an opportunity to work with children from the Windmill School every Wednesday morning and so, during their final three years in school (13–16 age group) the Lady

Adrian children experience a total of one and a half terms working with children who are profoundly handicapped; ii. that liaison with Chesterton Community College has produced two combined groups working in a special modular GCSE course in which our type of approach to PE now plays an important role. This last point has the advantage of giving the work the kudos of examination curriculum status and so helps to ensure its continuation in the future; iii. that as part of the Community Sports Leader Award, a number of Sixth Form pupils now assist in a variety of PE lessons at the Lady Adrian. The experience can count towards their overall assessment or simply be a voluntary activity.

Second, Lady Adrian has now become a major resource for the local community as you can see from Figure 5.2. Third, the number of children who have been involved in the second and third phases is larger than one might think — 330 all told — a figure which includes children from every point on the continuum of physical ability, and a number which continues to grow as the groups continue to operate and new links are formed.

Setting up Links: Guidelines

The past two years, especially, have taught me quite a lot about the business of putting groups together and setting up links between schools. I have tried in the previous pages to share with you some of the problems I encountered. Now let me suggest a few guidelines which may help to circumvent those problems and make life a little smoother for you if you are thinking about creating similar groups or links:

1. *Recommending a child*: any teacher who wishes to recommend a child for inclusion in a DMD group must be clear in his or her own mind what is actually meant by DMD, so that he/she recommends only a child with genuine motor problems and not one whose difficulties lie elsewhere, e.g., in emotional disturbance or intellectual backwardness.

2. *Composing a group*: there must be a distinct gap either of age, or

physical ability, or of both, between the two sets of pupils who make up the DMD group. The introduction into these groups of children with behavioural problems need not pose special difficulties, but in these circumstances it is essential to make sure that there is both a significant chronological *and* physical ability gap between the groups, otherwise you run the risk of creating a situation where some smart alec will take advantage of circumstances and either slow down or interrupt progress altogether. The older or physically more able children must be taken into the teachers' confidence and be fully briefed on what will be expected of them.

3. *Rules*: make clear, simple rules for behaviour right from the start, so that the group can operate successfully with a minimum of interruption. Do not make too much fuss over breaches of these rules. Have a predesignated adult at hand to deal with the problem quickly and efficiently.

4. *Facilities and equipment*: the space in which your group will be working should be considered very carefully beforehand. Make sure that it is suitable for your requirements and that if you need to make changes or adaptations to your environment, the means of making those changes are available to you.

Plan each session, and do not forget to include such elementary considerations as how the two groups are going to get to the facility, how long it will take each to get there, how much time is required for setting up and taking down equipment, precisely what equipment is needed for this particular session, and so forth.

5. *Activities*: make sure the activities will balance out between what will work and what will need working on. The children must, in the main, *succeed* in every lesson and be allowed to realize that they have been successful in much of what they have been asked to do.

Finally, three brief observations. First, be aware that there is a danger of such groups becoming over-dependent on a single personality. Try to make sure that this does not happen. Second, a resource school works best within the limits of its local community. If you over-extend yourself you will start to do your job less well than you should, and the first people to suffer will be your own children from your own school. Third, developing links with other schools is immensely facilitated by the local grapevine. You do not necessarily have to go out and sell your ideas to relative strangers. Good news travels fast and if you build a successful group in your own school it will reach others very quickly and you will find yourself approached and asked to help set up new groups and new links in a remarkably short space of time.

Chapter 6

Looking to the Future

By now it should be clear that my observations in the previous chapters are heading towards a particular view or stance, and perhaps now is a good time to summarize and give further consideration to the suggestions I have been making. Fundamental to them all is the simple question: how should we evaluate children in physical terms?

My belief is that where possible we should move away from labelling them (which is a kind of stigmatization) and hiving them off into convenient 'handicap groups', (which only serves further to increase the stigmatization). This effectively isolates them and may be administratively convenient, but it does more harm than good, largely because *it reinforces our assumption that any child who is not self-evidently able-bodied is handicapped*. 'Handicap' is an awkward term, because its popular usage assumes a degree of physical inability which may well not be present. In other words, to use an exaggerated example, a child suffering from spina bifida is indeed handicapped: a clumsy child on the other hand is simply suffering from delayed motor development. Whatever the dictionaries say about 'handicap', popular psychology is too quick to use it of both these children, and this is the point at which I want adults to take a hard look both at their preconceptions and at individual children and ask themselves: 'Do I really mean this child is "handicapped", or do I mean something else?'. The honest approach to that will profoundly affect their whole subsequent approach and expectations.

Instead of thinking in generalities then, we need to start from the point of clearly establishing what abilities exist within each child and then working out how those abilities may be best utilized in physical activity. The consensus of opinion among all the adults who have played a part in the type of group I have been describing is that all children who participate, whether they are at the profoundly handicapped or the able-bodied end of the continuum of physical ability, derive tremendous benefit from planned activity, with significant improvements in their physical development, mental awareness and academic work, and also enhanced self-image, self-esteem and self-confidence.

If we are to change our perceptions of what constitutes physical status in a child, we must also change our idea about the status of PE within a school. Since the physical development of an individual is likely to be intimately bound up with his or her emotional, social and intellectual development, the role of PE within our own educational system must be seen as crucial rather than tangential. But we must be careful to get our priorities right. Any programme of physical activity aiming to be developmental in its approach should satisfy four clear objectives:

  i. general motor ability
  ii. physical fitness
  iii. psychosocial adjustment
  iv. emotional adjustment (see Miller and Sullivan, 1982).

Any attempt to fulfil these requirements, however, must constantly and consistently refer back to motor development, for it is this area which is the core of physical development and underpins all the other PE aims. Weighting lessons in favour of physical fitness alone is a distorted approach, although it is one which is all too common in our schools, and is undoubtedly not the best way of satisfying the needs of any given group. Balance between the demands of our various declared aims and objectives must be our approach. Where all four aims are given our full attention, with none assuming precedence over the others, there we find progress for all and not just for some. The magic word is *equilibrium*.

Something else which should not be neglected, of course, is the emphasis upon mainstreaming made by the 1981 Education Act. This says that where possible, children with special educational needs should have those needs met in their local community school, a requirement which unfortunately for many children does not work out in practice, largely because of the psychological attitudes of children (low self-esteem, etc.) and of adults (compartmentalization) to which we have drawn attention.

Much of the research on mainstreaming has taken place in America as a result of the 'Right to Education Campaign', fought by the parents of children with special educational needs in the early 1970s, the turning point of which came as a result of *The Pennsylvania Case* (1971). This case established that every 'impaired' or 'handicapped' youth had the right to a free public (i.e., state) education, whatever his or her degree of retardation; that each child had to be provided with an individual educational programme tailored to suit his or her specific needs; and that the education should take place in the least-restricted environment, i.e., in the local mainstream school. From this came *Public Law, 94-142 — Education for all Handicapped Children Act of 1975*. Six major points are mandated by law:

1. Equal educational opportunity.
2. Education in the least restrictive environment.
3. Recommended extension of school age to 3–21.
4. Development of an individualized education plan written by a multidisciplinary team for each child.
5. Parental involvement in diagnosis and programme planning as of right.
6. Responsibility for compliance on the states and local education agencies (Miller and Sullivan, 1982, p. 5).

One can make a number of observations about these points, some positive, others negative. On the positive side, one notes that the Americans have adopted a strong moral position on the education of children with restricted physical ability, and have therefore taken steps to achieve real changes in the educational system. There is a sentiment here with which I fully concur: 'No one who finds pleasure in it should be excluded from the satisfaction of a physical movement' (Miller and Sullivan, 1982, p. 56. Note the indefinite article).

Those whom they quantify as impaired, they have tried,

supported by legislation, to integrate in regular classes; and they have also adopted PE programmes in the most painstaking fashion, tailoring them to suit a whole variety of individual cases, so that this mainstreaming can take place with very widely based advantage. Recent census figures reveal that 45–48 million school children aged 6–17 in the United States, (or about 1 in 8) are rated as 'impaired'. This is a remarkable figure when one takes into account what the Americans seem to mean by 'impaired'.

On the negative side, however, one can point to possible ambiguity about the meaning of 'impaired'. Official figures seem to indicate that 'impaired' means 'quantifiably handicapped', i.e. blind, deaf, crippled, mentally retarded, etc. (Miller and Sullivan, 1982, pp. 3–4) which places such children on the far end of our continuum of physical ability. It does not appear to include DMD cases, and therefore one must ask oneself whether the carefully adopted programmes for the 'impaired' actually extend to those we in this country would designate 'clumsy'. Moreover, there is evidence to suggest that their profoundly handicapped children are directed towards special care schools rather than mainstreamed, and this in itself must restrict their learning environment, the very thing they do not need, since the 'least restrictive alternative' should be the aim of any attempt to deal with handicap. In addition, there is no evidence, as far as I can see, that the able-bodied are physically educated alongside the physically disabled (op. cit., p. 7). In general terms, then, it does not seem as though DMD children are either identified or catered for.

It is interesting to compare this American legislation with our own 1981 Education Act, which relates entirely to the provision of special education in England and Wales. The Act makes several points: 1. that Local Education Authorities must, under certain given circumstances, make sure that children with special educational needs are given the opportunity to be mainstreamed; 2. that parents of such children play an active participatory role in assessing what the special needs of their children are; 3. that teachers (or other professionally-qualified adults) be made aware of these needs and play their part in ensuring that those needs are met and satisfied; 4. that it is the duty of the Local Education Authority to make sure that the provisions of the Act are carried out (Section 2, subsections 2, 3 and 7). In other words, the underlying intention is to point the Local Education Authority in the direction of mainstreaming in a manner somewhat similar to that of the American Act, and one's immediate reaction is to applaud the positive strides which the British Act makes towards raising the profile of special needs in education.

Second thoughts, however, raise a question. How far does it really measure up to its main principle: that provision for children with special needs should be integrated into the main flow of local education? Let us look more closely at the actual wording of subsection 2 and 3:

> 2. Where a Local Education Authority arranges special education provision for a child for whom they maintain a statement under section 7 of this Act, it shall be the duty of the authority, *if the conditions mentioned in subsection (3) below are satisfied*, that he is educated in an ordinary school.
> 3. *The conditions* are that account has been taken, in accordance with section 7, of the views of the child's parents and *that educating the child within the ordinary school is compatible* with:
>   (a) his receiving the special education that he requires
>   (b) the provision of efficient education for the children with whom he will be educated
>   (c) the efficient use of resources.
>
> (emphasis added)

The word 'if' means that the Act's principle of integration rests, in fact, upon certain conditions. If they are met, integration should, indeed must, take place; if they are not, it will not.

Now, this may appear niggling and unreasonable, but what the Act seems quite clearly to imply is that a child's needs will have to be of a specific, easily apprehensible nature in order to fulfil the conditions it lays down. He will have to be ambulant, able to communicate (if only somewhat), emotionally stable; he will have to be lucky enough to encounter special needs expertise in a mainstream school; he will cause minimum disruption to the other children in the school; the school itself must not need to undergo major reconstruction or provide lots of new equipment.

This is beginning to sound just a mite cynical, but let us be realistic. Any Local Education Authority faced with a sudden shift towards integration has three choices: 1. to embrace the notion wholeheartedly *and fund it*; 2. to maintain its current special needs provision through its special schools, i.e., maintain segregation, or 3. (probably the most popular) to make sure that MLD children are integrated within mainstream schools, but continue special provision for those who are self-evidently disabled. Now if an LEA adopts the first solution, everything is fine; but if the second or third solutions obtain, there is need for action by local parents or teachers. Without integration, DMD children who are already in mainstream schools and, as we have seen, form a more or less invisible group within a largely able-bodied community, will, in all likelihood, continue to wrestle with their problems unnoticed and unassisted. Add the presence of disadvantaged children from special schools, however, and the awareness of staff, pupils and parents alike is likely to be heightened, with the result that many of the invisible children start to be visible, their needs, being known, can start to be catered for, and thus the whole continuum of ability, not just the two extremes and occasional grade between, receives appropriate attention.

Physical Education, therefore, provides not just *a* starting point for action, if action be needed, but *the* starting point, since it is the one subject which is capable of integrating children across the whole spectrum of ability (and in large numbers) and can do this much better, much more easily and much more efficiently than any other. It is not enough simply to have children with special needs in your primary school or comprehensive school, and section 2, subsection (7) of the Act tells us quite clearly why:

> *Where a child who has special educational needs is being educated in an ordinary school* maintained by the Local Education Authority *it shall be the duty of those concerned with making special education provision for that child to secure*, so far as is both compatible with the objectives mentioned in paragraphs (a) to (c) of subsection (3) and

reasonably practicable, *that the child engages in the activities of the school together with children who do not have special educational needs.*

(emphasis added)

There are many examples within the book of those barriers being overcome and there is no reason why any of the specialist activities and support groups I have described earlier should not exist in many, if not all, of our mainstream schools.

The 1981 Act was followed by another in 1988. What is the Education Reform Act aiming to do? What are its priorities and its emphases? A glance at the actual wording of the Act is, once again, informative. Its clauses on the general aims of the curriculum, for example, are as broad as the Ganges, aiming to promote 'the spiritual, moral, cultural, mental and physical development of pupils at the school and of society and to prepare such pupils for the opportunities, responsibilities and experiences of adult life' (Section 1, subsections 2 [a] and [b]). Religious education must be provided 'for all registered pupils at the school' (Section 2, subsection 1 [a]): and as far as Wales is concerned, Welsh must be a core subject in Welsh speaking schools, and a foundation subject in non-Welsh speaking schools, (Section 3, subsections 1 [b] and 2 [c]). So religion must be available to all, and in Wales, singled out in the Act for special consideration, for obvious reasons, Welsh too must be made available to all.

Here then we have attitudes which are positive and non-discriminatory. Access to subjects deemed desirable — I have selected religious education and Welsh as examples — *must* be provided by schools and their local authorities. But what are we to make of the other clauses in the Act, clauses which are not so positive, not so encouraging? On the one hand, religious education must be provided for all registered pupils at the school (subsection 1[a]), and on the other, 'subsection 1(a) above shall not apply in the case of a maintained special school'. Why not? What happened suddenly to access? The words 'not apply' and 'modification' begin to recur over and over again in the Act: subsection 16 (a) and (b), subsection 17 (a) and (b), subsection 19 (a) all use the words, legitimately, of course, since no one is suggesting that special cases do not arise and do not need special consideration. However, let us look at all these 'negatives' a little more closely because they have implications, serious implications, for the special school.

Let us take the example of a special school and the curriculum it is capable of offering. Smaller staff numbers, limited equipment and lack of specialist facilities will automatically exclude its pupils from many areas of the National Curriculum unless they can tap into their local comprehensives and share their resources. This means, on the one hand, science laboratories, workshops, gymnasia, swimming pools, the physical resources which the special school may not have or may have but poorly equipped or under funded. But on the other, it refers also to the academic curriculum of the comprehensive, since some of the special school children may be capable of tackling GCSE subjects not on offer in their own school and will need, and ought to have access to, the teaching expertise available to the comprehensive pupil.

All these resources, whether they be people or equipment or buildings, are expensive and the comprehensive is now, according to the Act, to be responsible for running its own budget. Is it not perfectly possible, in the real world of real teaching, real budgets, real schools, that faced with pressures of operating the National Curriculum, Local Management of their own schools, meeting Attainment Targets and National Testing, the head teacher may decide that cooperation, access, availability, call it what you will, is rather too expensive in terms of money, time, teachers and other resources, and so will close the shutters, lock the doors and bar the gates (so to speak) in order to concentrate on his or her own school, leaving the children from special schools to sink or swim? The fact that Section 17 (a) can disapply the National Curriculum and that Section 18 (a) can deny the application of the National Curriculum to statemented pupils might well provide our colleagues in mainstream with a convenient argument, should they feel they need one, to go it alone and leave us to make our own way home. In other words the legislation leaves the special schools toothless, yet again, in the drive towards normalization of the educational needs of the statemented child. As Klaus Weddell (1988) observed: 'As far as pupils with special educational needs are concerned there is still a very long way to go. For these pupils and their parents, the passing of the 1981 Act represented the beginning of a statutory commitment to meeting their needs which the Education Reform Bill as presented to Parliament has done nothing to confirm'. This comment was made prior to the 1988 Act's becoming law, but one is still left with the feeling that the fight for the right of access to as much of the National Curriculum as each special needs child can cope with has to be won all over again, some eight years after the 1981 Act was passed. 'Shall not apply' and 'modifications', far from being the timely and careful provisions which, no doubt, the government intended, may turn out, under the multifarious pressures of daily educational existence, to be loopholes through which those good intentions escape and disappear, in which case, the state of the special schools is no better than before. Indeed, I should say it was worse; for it is a parlous thing for the working of good intentions to rest upon nothing more firm that the sands of goodwill.

Play — Game — Sport

Before we go on to discuss the role of PE within the new National Curriculum, it will be as well to get straight what we mean by the terms 'play', 'game' and 'sport', since these and the phrase 'Physical Education' itself tend to be bandied about both in print and in conversation without the users' or listeners' being fully aware of the implications of what is being said. So let me put this as simply as possible.

Physical Education consists of the acquisition and development of efficient motor function. Efficient motor function is acquired through play which may be a solo or a social experience; efficient motor function is developed through play and movement experience which may or may not use equipment.

The words *play* and *game* are not synonymous. The concept 'game' always involves other people, i.e., social play, whereas the concept 'play' embraces solo as well as social experience. Therefore 'play' includes 'game', but 'game' does not constitute 'play'. One must be careful here not to be led astray by the notion 'playing games', because 'playing' here is part of a verb, and 'games' is a plural concrete noun, whereas the *play* and *game* I am discussing here are abstract nouns, concepts not 'things'.

The words *game* and *sport*, on the other hand, are synonymous because they both involve the notion of competition and competition takes place between two or more people. Hence 'game' and 'sport' necessarily imply 'social play' as opposed to 'solo play'. Once again, the concept 'sport' should not be confused with 'sports' which is, like games, a plural concrete noun. Thus play is both solo and social. As a solo performance it is not 'game' or 'sport', but as a social performance, it is.

Acquiring efficient motor function initially through play must be done as both a solo and a social experience with the balance biased towards the latter. Now, it might be argued that since social play necessarily involves competition, a DMD child will have his/her inadequacies highlighted thereby and in consequence will find the experience distressing and unhelpful. This is an argument for withdrawal for individual treatment. The counter-argument is that every child must be given opportunities (and I stress the plural) to exercise physical power and thus manipulate other people's performances. This is because exercise of physical power under these circumstances (a) gives pleasure to the individual exercising it; (b) helps to develop a skill or skills during the exercise; and (c) increases legitimate self-esteem. 'Power' and 'manipulate' are emotive words and must not be misunderstood in this context. The Latin word for power, potentia, refers to ability; he/she is able to do something because he/she has the power or control to do it. Manipulation is not necessarily undesirable. Being a team leader involves manipulation, for example, but that is not a negative and therefore undesirable role. But if we take it at its worst in the context of play, we could see manipulation as cheating. My experience of giving children a relatively free hand in lessons is that whenever someone begins to manipulate others in this negative fashion, his peers start to object and then to isolate him from participation in the social play, and thus he learns from his peers that negative manipulation is undesirable. It can be quite important, incidentally, for the teacher in charge to let this happen, rather than jump in at once as the supreme arbiter of moral standards. The lesson is underlined for the child if he/she learns it in course of play from other children rather than by means of superior diktat.

But it can be argued that withdrawal for individual treatment gives a chance for the child to exercise unlimited physical power over him/herself, and so (a) (b) and (c) above will be fulfilled. What then is the peculiar benefit of social play? It is perfectly true that withdrawal often works with certain children. The greatest drawback of solo play, however, is that it gives the child no opportunity of measuring his/her own progress against the progress (or lack of progress) of other children, and so an important stimulus to encouragement and self-improvement is lost. One might also add that social play offers a greater chance for variety in activity and so increases the element of fun. Fun must not be underestimated. Fun stops PE from being a drudgery and if the child looks forward to PE because he/she finds it fun, an important psychological battle has been won.

Game and *sport*, then, are social play. A game, games, a sport, sports are concrete examples of the abstract concept game/ sport = social play. This has important consequences for the way in which we think, speak and write about Physical Education:

a. Physical Education is the acquisition and development of efficient motor function through play.
b. Games and sports (football, swimming, dance, gymnastics, athletics, etc.) are simply individual examples of play.
c. Therefore any *one* of these can be a legitimate way of acquiring and developing efficient motor function, i.e., any *one* can provide what is known as Physical Education.

Notice that I said 'can' provide, not should. Variety of experience is important. My point is that it is not important for the reasons people usually give. Let me illustrate this with two pieces of evidence, one published material, the other anecdotal.

First, *Physical Education 5–16* (DES, 1989). This guide to the requirements of the National Curriculum in PE lists specific key areas of physical education — gymnastics, dance, games, swimming, outdoor pursuits, athletics — and goes on to list further desirable targets a child should have achieved at certain ages. It strikes me that what the document assumes is a) that competence in the separate disciplines of gym and dance, etc., is what every child should aim at; b) that the separate disciplines have distinctive individual qualities and demands which make that discipline qualitatively different from others; c) that ultimately the aim of PE is to turn a child into a gymnast, a dancer, a footballer, a swimmer, etc.; d) if the aim of c) is not achieved, that child's physical education has been in some measure a 'failure'. I say this because I have the strongest possible impression that the document has taken as its goal the notion of competence in a given area of physical activity (games or sports) and worked out the sequence of desired physical skills which will ultimately satisfy that particular notion of physical activity. In other words, physical education = training for games/sports.

If, however, I am right in suggesting that PE = acquisition and development of efficient motor function through play, then a document which purports to set out a sequence of developmental desiderata should begin with the notion of play (i.e., play solo + play = game/sport) and work its way forward through a whole range of physical activities which are seen as of equal importance because all are seen as play.

To illustrate the implication of this point, let me turn to an anecdote. A large comprehensive school (fictitious — my example is based on a selection of many, it is not a portrait of one) has what it regards as a fairly enlightened approach to PE. There is mixed PE throughout the school, plenty of team sports, a variety of clubs, an enthusiastic PE staff, a supportive head teacher. The head of boys PE is keen on promoting basketball. He is a good player himself and hopes to encourage interest among the children. The school caters for dance which is taught by the head of girls PE. She wants him to teach dance as well: he is reluctant. Why? There are three reasons: i. dance is all very well as a physical activity, but it is really for girls, not boys; ii. he himself is not very good at dance and is sure he would not teach it well; iii. he can fulfil all the requirements of the National

Curriculum through basketball, so why should he take on dance which is superfluous to his pupils' requirements?

We may ignore i. as self evidently silly, but it is worth making the point that although this attitude is officially outdated, it still informs a remarkably large number of teachers coming into the profession, though few would be willing to admit it openly, of course. Point ii., however, is important because it suggests a common motivation for taking up PE as a job: 'I am good at games and especially at basketball. Therefore I shall become a PE teacher and specialize in basketball'. Thus a person enters the profession intent upon passing on his/her own preoccupation with games which he/she happens to be good at, and intent also upon producing clones to continue the process. The teacher is at the far end of the ability continuum and his motivation gears him to deal most effectively with those children who occupy that end of the continuum too. Others elsewhere on the continuum who do not or cannot match the expectations promoted by the teacher's motivation are inevitably regarded, even if only subconsciously, as 'failures'. This is where inability or unwillingness to distinguish between game and games, sport and sports can lead. This is certainly where a misconception of the meaning of physical education leads.

The cult of 'games' and of 'team spirit' which has informed British PE ever since Victorian times appears to have had a lasting effect. 'Competition' and 'competitiveness' are often treated as though they were dirty words, and solo performance is sometimes emphasized at the expense of social play. My point is that if PE is seen as physical development through play, and not as training for games, a balance can be struck between play (solo) and play (social) so that each receives its due emphasis as a desirable part of the overall acquisition of efficient motor function. It is important that one child's ability to tie a shoelace, button a coat, use a knife and fork be seen as equal in value to another child's ability to dribble a ball, shoot for goal, and contribute to the work of a team. There is no innate virtue in one form of play over another.

But what of the idea that if basketball can fulfil the National Curriculum requirements, there is no need to take on additional subjects? Is the man correct? The answer, in the light of what I have been saying earlier, is yes. If PE is the acquisition and development of efficient motor function, any one example of play can, if properly taught, provide all that is required. The fact that it can, however, does not mean to say that it should. I have mentioned before the advantages of variety in play, and we must take into account two additional things: inclination and the application of efficient motor function (EMF) in terms of skills. Put simply, basketball is not everyone's cup of tea. Swimming, dance, athletics, etc. have their attractions and each child should have the opportunity to participate in the game he/she personally finds attractive. The word 'access' comes back from our earlier discussion. Secondly, what is acquisition and development of EMF for? The answer is 'living efficiently with a measure of legitimate self-esteem'. But it may well be that 'living efficiently' includes, or will come to include, a measure of social play manifested in specific examples — *a* game, *a* sport. Participation in this requires the exercise of EMF through particular skills, and therefore the acquisition and development of those skills becomes desirable. But acquisition and development of skills for basketball alone is a sterile exercise if one's inclination runs towards swimming or dance. So access to a variety of games is again important.

At the risk of labouring my point, however, let me state it once again. Physical Education is not the same as training for games. It is the acquisition and development of EMF through play. Once that basic concept is realised and accepted, it changes one's whole attitude towards physical activity and the consequences for PE in schools are enormous. It represents a break with the past, a cutting loose from the psychological and social preconceptions of the past which still largely inform those who direct and those who carry out our physical education. Misunderstanding of what should be the basic aims of PE, misconceptions of basic terminology, produce schemes for the future which leave a large sector of the school population out in the cold, and help to perpetuate the notion — widely if subconsciously accepted not only by LEAs and head teachers but also by PE practitioners themselves — that PE means 'playing games' and is therefore inferior to other parts of the curriculum. 'Playing games' quite possibly is. 'Acquiring and developing efficient motor function' most certainly is not.

New Initiatives

The 1988 Education Reform Act has certainly enlivened the working atmosphere in schools the length and breadth of England and Wales, and woe betide the teacher who has not followed closely its development alongside TVEI, TRIST, GRIST, CPVE, GCSE, etc. Of all these innovations perhaps the two most significant are the GCSE and TVEI, (Technical and Vocational Education Initiative) because not only do they seek to influence the content of the schools' curriculum, but also the way the curriculum is taught. In the case of some subjects, the changes consequent upon the new developments are fundamental. History, for example, must now lay greater stress upon the acquisition of specific skills: understanding, appreciation and ability to deploy documentation, for example, and the process of problem-solving rather than the acquisition of a coherent body of historical knowledge, chronologically delivered. So what are the implications for PE? How does it fit into the new curriculum; and what is the place for special groups in the new regime?

I have tried to make two points clear so far in the general trend of the book. First, PE is an essential part of the education of every individual from the profoundly handicapped to the fully able-bodied. Secondly, mutual assistance by individuals and groups along the whole continuum of physical ability is indeed mutual. The able-bodied person who helps someone less able than himself receives benefit from his partner. It is a venture of cooperation and co-benefaction, not a process which works only one way, *de haut en bas*. But as far as the specific question about involvement in GCSE as opposed to the whole school curriculum is concerned, a slightly different answer needs to be, and can be, given.

As far as the academic side of things is concerned, PE offers a wide variety of areas for study — anatomy, physiology, hygiene, the history of sport, etc. — and these will provide a whole range of assessable topics for testing and evaluating by means of written papers. But PE can also be used in quite a different fashion, related to the second of my general points; and here I can best illustrate what I am saying by referring to a particular case, a Special Groups Module of the GCSE Community Studies at one of Lady Adrian's link schools, Chesterton Community College.

The course is made up of six modules with 100 per cent coursework, and this is how it worked last academic year (1988–9):

1. You and your community
2. Myself
3. Special groups*
4. Healthy living
5. Community health and safety
6. Leisure and recreation.

*The aim of this module is to develop an awareness of one particular group within the community that has been identified as having special needs. It is hoped candidates will develop a positive attitude by having direct experience of working with such a group. Candidates can choose from one of the following: the elderly, children with learning difficulties, people with mental and/or physical handicaps, or other groups identified as having special needs.

Content

1. *Definition of the term 'special needs'*. Pupils should be able to gain an understanding of their particular problems. They should show an appreciation of the factors which contribute to physical, social and mental disability, including genetic disorder, accidental injury, drug abuse and disease.

2. *The needs of and provision for special groups*. Pupils will be expected to have a knowledge of the statutory and voluntary provision for special groups. They should be able to discuss society's attitude to these groups.

3. *Practical involvement*. Possible methods of assessment for this module:

    i. placement diary — actual work experience
   ii. placement report
  iii. child study
   iv. design a practical aid.

There were two parallel groups operating this course. Each was to be linked with an SLD school within the local community in an activity that would allow either one-to-one relationships or, in some cases where the children were profoundly handicapped, two-to-one. Both these groups were to operate for one term only, as required by the modular approach. Group A was led by a teacher from the special school and Group B by a teacher and a welfare assistant from a second special school.

Group A was involved in the employment of the Halliwick Swimming techniques with the special group at their own community college pool. Many opportunities were taken not only to encourage the children in individual activities but also to play group games involving singing and noise making which at all times maintained close physical contact between the able and the less able.

Group B travelled to a nearby SLD school and combined the activities of Veronica Sherbourne and Walli Meier, a good blend of relationship play and movement with music. Here again the children worked one-to-one, two-to-one and combined in large group activities, all with a healthy level of physical 'busyness' and physical contact. As the weeks went by the mainstream children in both groups were encouraged to create or bring new activities to the sessions.

If this sort of thing now sounds familiar to you, it is because it is a natural development of those links which had already been established during the past three years. Five schools altogether were involved in these modules, sharing facilities, expertise, equipment, ideas, participants and above all an enormous amount of human interaction which was mutually beneficial to all. The physical experience for the mainstream children, though somewhat daunting at first, contributed much to their understanding of what it must be like to be physically unable, and this understanding was clearly illustrated in the quality and quantity of academic work which the experience inspired. It all goes to show that special groups such as these support one's conviction that not only do mainstream and special schools benefit from these mutual links, but that they actually *need* each other. The sessions were of immense value, in terms of more activity, more stimulus, and sheer hard work, to the special children and the fact that, due to pupil interest and desire, both groups continued beyond their allotted time into the next term, was a statement of how much value the mainstream school placed upon this way of working. Moreover, this module has now been written into the GCSE Community Studies course at Chesterton, as a permanent fixture.

As far as TVEI and PE are concerned, I think it is enough to make the general point. 'Communication skills' are receiving and are about to receive a good deal of emphasis, and the point I wish to make is that it is important we do not fall into the trap of thinking — 'Communications skills – computers – intelligent operator – = able bodied)'. These subconscious linkages are all too easy to formulate, but if we do make them, we run the risk of depriving the children in special schools of access to the full range of opportunities which are bound to be made available in mainstream. Remember (to take a couple of extreme examples just to underline my point) the communication skills of Professor Stephen Hawking or Christie Nolan. The lesson they teach is obvious. *No one* is beyond communication, and in consequence let us remember to assume that all new educational initiatives are actually for all: the inclusive, not exclusive, frame of mind.

Assessment and Testing

The notion of assessment and testing has proved to be one of the most contentious areas of all the new initiatives. But whether one approves of such testing or not, the fact is that at some stage, PE will join all the other subjects at school in being weighed in the balance of each child's educational progress. Will this pose problems for children in special schools? Hardly: these children are already tested in several ways, for example, by the TOMI (Test of Motor Impairment) to which I have referred earlier (see page 26), and these tests are straightforward diagnostic tools used by physiotherapists in their assessment of what range of prescriptive treatments will be appropriate in each case. Morever, these tests are used periodically to monitor those children who are deemed to need physiotherapists' support.

Testing, however, is often seen in a negative light. The TOMI, for example, is a test of motor impairment and because children assessed by it are compared with a pre-conceived standard 'norm', there is actually an inbuilt failure rate in many such tests of 5 per cent. So, yes, a test is useful in that it identifies children who are failing in one aspect or another of their physical development, but 'children who are failing' must not, because of a test, be converted into 'failures' and treated accordingly. Testing must be seen only in a positive light and be accompanied by the constant presence of safety nets along the lines I have described earlier, so that they are not stigmatized as failures, but
on the contrary, may be directed into situations which will give them opportunities for progress, success, and enhancement of legitimate self-esteem.

> With its curriculum, a school has to decide on long and short term goals; on sequences of progression, including progression in terms of concept formation and development; attitudes; ideas; knowledge and skills. The need for flexibility and for matching tasks to the individual implies that sequences of goals in different curriculum areas may vary in respect of needs of individuals and groups. It is very important for teachers to have a clear idea of progression in all aspects of the curriculum, and to use this for evaluating progress. It is on this basis for assessing the progress of all children, that it is possible to become aware of children who have special educational needs. *The Fish Report* (ILEA, 1985 para. 2.7.6).

Chapter 7

The People Involved with the Theory

What then of Donald, Annabel, Anne and Sean, three years on since we last met them in Chapter 3, and now aged 16, 14, 13, and 15 respectively? If what I have been saying throughout this book actually works in practice, not only on the physical but also on the psychological well-being of all these children, they should have improved appreciably.

As far as the former is concerned we have reason to be pleased. Donald, Anne and Sean no longer need the support of the physiotherapist; Annabel's particular medical condition leaves her left side going in and out of spasm, so she will continue to need help at least for a while longer. But what is especially worth noting is the way the attitude of all four towards physical activity has altered. Donald (pp. 37–9) is now waiting to begin his post-16 education at a residential college which specializes in his type of disability. He enters his next phase of life as a very good swimmer and more than keen footballer, willing and able to take part in all kinds of physical exertion. One relic of his earlier immaturity remains; he whinges when asked to run long distances. But that is hardly serious (don't we all whinge about something?) and his progress must be regarded as both pleasing and encouraging. Annabel, as I said, still needs support, but she never misses a PE session, always gives of her best, and thoroughly enjoys what she does. She actually gets an extra PE lesson each week so that she can help infant children, thus illustrating my point about the mutual benefits of links between schools. Anne (p. 42) has improved beyond recognition in all areas of her physical development and is currently the best 800 m. runner in the junior/middle part of the school. What is more, she actively enjoys it. Sean (pp. 43–4) has turned into a football fanatic who would like to spend his whole week playing and thinking about the game, and his enthusiasm expressed in talk is as important an indicator of his general improvement as his ability to play.

This all sounds rather like an end of term report doesn't it? 'Has worked well and made generally satisfactory progress. A pleasing year's work'. Individual cases, however, tell us a good deal about how any remedial process works in practice, and such illustrations also enable the reader to pick up points peculiarly relevant to his or her own experience: 'We have a boy just like Sean', 'Anne reminds me of Katy', 'John is rather like Donald in some ways'. Let me offer you three more case studies, not repetitious of those you have read already, but three which can illustrate somewhat different points about the relationship between school and physiotherapist, one school and another, and the role of parents in helping to help their child.

Case E: Roberta, aged 8 years.
Problems: Shy, introverted, non-doer with poor recording skills, crumbles under pressure.

Initially Roberta was very apprehensive when she was referred to Lady Adrian School by the physiotherapist to join the motor skills group, and for the first few sessions her mother came along too. Soon however, Roberta felt somewhat reassured. The pace of our lessons was not overwhelming, the noise level was not aggressively high, the children taking part seemed to be having fun, so she started to join in. Two activities particularly appealed to her during these initial stages: the 'naming' process advocated by Walli Meier (p. 18) and Tags, whose value, by the way, can scarcely be overstated. Roberta has now been with the group for a whole year, and has improved almost beyond recognition. From being shy, introverted and a non-doer, she has turned into a confident (even brash) young miss who is more lively and more able than she herself realized she could be. She will remain with the group through next year, and as a result of the benefical effects, which have become apparent at her mainstream school, Lady Adrian has been asked to provide a similar kind of support for her literacy skills.

It all goes to show not just that this sort of remedial process works, but that cooperation between mainstream and special schools can catch children who might otherwise pass through their mainstream careers largely unnoticed — 'the invisible children', to return to a phrase I used earlier in the book — and offer them a way out of their predicament, a way to escape stigmatization and a way towards integration with their peers. Maintaining the mainstream placement when it might be tempting to go for statementing and placing Roberta in a special school, actually makes economic sense according to the 1986 figures, which show that the annual average cost of a special school place is £4,444, compared with £897 for primary schools (see Jones, 1989: 3).

Case F: Jemima, aged 12 years.

This is a case in which the physiotherapy service was not involved. I happened to be observing Jemima's dance lesson in her mainstream comprehensive and noticed that she was clearly at a disadvantage with respect to others in the group because of her poor motor development. When I pointed this out to the school, I was told that Jemima was also having problems in her academic work. Concentration and speed of taking notes were two particular areas in which she was performing poorly. Her mother quickly appreciated the point about motor difficulties and asked what could be done, and this led to Jemima's being referred to the Lady Adrian School. Once again the familiar story of amelioration in both performance and self-esteem follows, and although there is still some way to go with her physical remediation, nothing could be better than her psychological progress. Pleasure in performing, striving to achieve, ability to stick with the task in hand — these are all measured improvements achieved during the two terms she has been with the Lady Adrian group.

One point about this example is that Jemima's disabilities were not picked up by a physiotherapist but by a PE teacher. One does not *have* to wait for and rely upon intervention of external specialist expertise to notice DMD. Provided one has some basic information about motor function and remembers to keep one's eyes open during lessons, another invisible child can become visible and so avoid unnecessary retardation in his or her physical development and welfare.

The other point is the involvement of Jemima's mother. Parents can be enormously supportive: Roberta's mother for example, actually changed her job so that she could be available regularly to transport her daughter the long distance between her junior school and Lady Adrian. Another illustration of parental involvement and support appears in the words of the father of my last example.

Case G: Patrick, aged 15 years.

> For the first ten years of Patrick's school life, we knew what his school reports were going to say well before they actually arrived. No matter what the subject. The reports always told us that he was a 'likeable lad' who 'always tried hard' and that, when it came to the bit about his classroom behaviour, he was 'a credit to his class'.
>
> Unfortunately, when the reports got on to his academic qualities, his teachers seemed a little preoccupied with what he couldn't do rather than with what he could. Comments such as 'lacks concentration', 'lets his mind wander', 'more care needed', 'clumsy' and 'handwriting very messy' were only to be expected because he was, unfortunately, guilty on all counts.
>
> Parents' evenings were a revelation. We used to have the customary small talk with his teachers, but once the real conversation started and we asked for opinions as to why this teacher or that teacher thought Patrick was like he was, no one could ever give us what seemed like a logical answer in that it rarely agreed with anyone else's opinion. The one thing they all did agree upon was that his coordination was bad.
>
> The frustration this caused us over the years was incredible. We knew something was not quite right but nobody seemed to be able to tell us what it was or where to go for help. We took him to see a specialist who gave him a thorough examination. He told us that Patrick's problems

were only minor and that as he grew older, he would learn to compensate for them in other ways.

While this was all going on, his academic work was suffering because once he had gone to the secondary school, he needed to write very quickly. That was something he simply could not do. He was given a broadside from all quarters and told to get his work looking neater. He could do this but his output dropped dramatically as a direct result. More broadsides came his way which meant that the vicious circle surrounded him still further and was becoming impossible to break.

I suspect this is not altogether an uncommon story. Once the parents got to know that the case was not hopeless or unfathomable, however, they were quick and eager to take positive steps to get their son appropriate assistance. Just as important, Patrick himself became fired with the notion that he was not after all doomed forever to come last in everything. His father describes the results of seven weeks' work:

His vocabulary and conversation at home have started to improve. He has started to express an opinion instead of just commenting.

He can hold a spanner and take the wheels off his cycle. This has always been a complete mystery to him.

The way he walks has changed. Gone is the characteristic shuffle. He now walks positively and does not find so many 'matchsticks' to fall over.

His stamina has improved out of all proportion. He now enjoys mowing the quarter of an acre of lawn and spending an hour walking up and down the garden in control of the power mower. Seven weeks ago the mower would have taken him, and in any event, he did not stick at it for more than 10 minutes at a time. Consequently, what was a piece of hard labour has turned into something he enjoys. He can run further without a break than he has ever done before and his general physical strength has increased considerably.

His confidence is starting to grow and he seems more aware of himself in general.

He says that he feels better in himself and I think he is just beginning to feel the control he is starting to get over parts of his own body that, until now, seem to have had a mind of their own.

As a summary, the past seven weeks have not only been an enjoyable experience for Patrick, they have taken a lot of frustration out of our house. At last someone is actually doing something positive and telling us all what Patrick can achieve. Not what he hasn't. We all know that there is still work to be done, but there is a light at the end of the tunnel, and it's a tunnel we are all happy to go through, especially Patrick.

Parents, then, are important. They have a major role to play in assisting the educationist in the process of a child's remediation, and satisfaction in the home helps to reinforce confidence at school so that the child does not pass from an atmosphere of success and high expectations into one of doubt and resigned low expectations. 'Nothing succeeds like success' is perfectly true and even more true, if that is possible, when expectation of success informs the circumambient atmosphere.

Conclusion

We have nearly finished; my principal points have been made, but there are still one or two things to be said that merit attention. Looking after special needs, integrating all but the most severely handicapped children into mainstream schools, providing suitable programmes for the DMD pupils, ensuring that all children, in fact, have the right to movement — all this involves large numbers of individuals whose roles in the process will be quite different, and produce certain consequences of which we must be aware. Integration is a fine aim, but one institution cannot be expected to cater for all the special needs of special needs children unless certain conditions are met. So let us be realistic: let us aim to do what we can and as much as we can with the schools we actually have at the present time. Providing support groups in our own schools and creating community links are the two most vital pieces of foundation work, and these have been the principal themes of my book. Let us suppose then, that you wish to become actively involved in this work and that you find yourself more or less in the position I was in when I started. What general pieces of advice can I give you, and what general comments can I make?

Remember that any Headteacher must be willing to support changes within his/her system, and that all those called on to implement the changes must have a clear understanding of why those changes ought to happen and how they are to be carried out. Headteachers are frequently bombarded by pet projects. If they are to accept and encourage changes in the school, they must be persuaded that those changes are capable of providing a solid respectable base from which all the children involved can benefit in the long term. The best way to persuade anyone of the long term benefits of anything is to actually present him/her with a series of short term, or even immediate successes, 'bait' so to speak, which will hook him or her upon your line and allow you to draw them into your creel at leisure. Do not be over-ambitious at the beginning. Think what can be done in *your* school with *your* children and *your* staff, and then go ahead and do it. Grander schemes and wider reaching plans can (and will) follow.

Here I address myself especially to those of you trained in PE: spend time with the severely disabled. People learn from looking at the extremes. PE teachers and students spend an awful lot of time with the able-bodied, and thus it becomes very difficult for them to make any radical psychological shift in their perceptions of what one means by the term 'physical ability'. Odd as it may sound at first, it is only by having some experience of disability that we can come to a deeper understanding of what ability is. I also think it important that every PE teacher should take a close look at the activity which he/she is directing at any given time. Is there a child who seems unable to cope with what you are asking him or her to do? Does the inability apply to the whole exercise or only part of it? What is the underlying cause of the disability? Do you actually understand what is wrong? Do you know what to do in order to start putting it right?

The ability to name every bone and muscle in the human body is not as important for the PE teacher as the capacity to recognize and understand the components of efficient motor function. Remember this when you next give a class instructions in the gymnasium or on the playing field. Asking a child to carry out a complex task is breath wasted if the child has a restricted base of skills. The components of motor function must *all* be developed, because a staged development of physical processes — sitting, tracking, etc., above all, sequencing — affects a child's mental and intellectual ability to make progress, for example, to follow instructions. What is more, each stage in this process must be successful before the next stage is attempted physically, so that physical and intellectual development proceed at a roughly equal rate. If the two fall out of sync, so to speak, the child becomes unbalanced. Case studies E, F, and G are all good examples of children whose all-round development is in a state of imbalance. Restoration of this balance is the key to their tremendous progress.

Attitude, therefore, is one of the keys to progress; and do remember that adult perceptions are of the first importance and are picked up very quickly by DMD children. If these children are made, even inadvertantly, to feel they are inadequate, they will rapidly manufacture ways of avoiding attention which assigns them failure or even just negatively expressed praise. Whenever the adults' psychology becomes positive in its approach, however, this ducking out and turning invisible ceases. So always set achievable targets and reinforce the children's success with positive physical and verbal praise. For example, a deformed hand should not be thrust out of sight and use, and treated as though it were useless. That is a negative approach. It must instead be brought into view, accepted, integrated with the rest of the body, and encouraged to do as much as it is capable of doing. That is a positive approach, and much more fruitful.

This in turn leads me to what I said at the beginning of Chapter 6 about such words as 'handicap'. If I label a child as 'cripple', 'clumsy', or 'backward', then that is what I shall get: a backward girl, a clumsy boy, a cripple. If I think instead 'continuum', what I shall get is an individual at a certain stage of a continuously moving process. That, after all, is what continuum means. It is not stationary: no one gets stuck at one point for ever; flow, progress, advance are the implications of such a process and if we think in these terms, we cannot help but think positively, and 'positive' does the trick.

The consequence of everything I have been saying is that PE must be seen as an *essential* component of every child's development from his/her earliest years. It must not be conceived in terms of 'an enjoyable way of spending Thursday afternoon', 'the only exercise they get', 'training to see who's good enough for the team'. Let me sing my tune just one more time. 'Game' is not the same as 'games', 'sport' is not 'sports' and PE does not consist of teaching the skills needed for games. Physical Education is the development of a child's efficient motor function. That is the foundation: everything else rests upon that.

Finally, let me address everyone. Every child should have the right to movement. It is not the exclusive concern of specialists, but the concern of everyone involved in any way in the process of education, that no child should be deprived of this right if his or her need can be seen or remedied. The 'seeing is all', and if what I have tried to say in this book has made it easier for more people to open their eyes and look more closely at what passes in front of them, I shall consider the book well done and my role as optician successful.

Appendix

Presented here are further examples of activities which will help bridge the 'gap' which exists between DMD children and the more able bodied. These are not lesson plans: they will not do your job for you. I have included them to provide a few starting-points from which you can develop your own lessons according to your particular skills, ideas and wishes.

1. Warm up games
2. Memory and sequencing games
3. Relays
4. Relationship plays
5. Rhythm and Rhyme games
6. Summer Circuits: adapted from ten step award scheme
7. Swimming for beginners
8. Ball games

Warm-up Games

Tunnel Tag — a Development of 'Stick in the Mud'

When caught, the child makes a 'tunnel', and holds the shape until released by another child's going through the tunnel.

Conditions A. Tunnel facing the floor
  Tunnel facing the ceiling
  Tunnel with 2 parts of the body touching the floor
  Tunnel with 3 parts of the body touching the floor
  Tunnel with 4 parts of the body touching the floor
 B. Released by someone going under, over, around or
  by a combination of two or three.
 C. Space, made smaller using lines in the floor.

Shape tag — varieties

When caught, the child makes a shape which has to be held until copied by another person.

Conditions A. Low shape, High shape, Long, Wide, Twisted; 1, 2, 3, 4 parts of body touching floor; Symmetrical/Asymmetrical shapes
 B. Release 'shape' by copying either by matching the shape, i.e. doing exactly the same, or by mirroring the shape.
 C. Space can be made smaller or irregular, using lines in the floor, with penalties for stopping outside the allotted areas, e.g. sit-ups, star jumps, press-ups.

Crab tag

All participants can only move by using both hands and feet. The game can be played face down or belly up. When caught, the crab has to freeze until released by another crab's sliding underneath.

Vault tag

When caught, the children must make a solid base on hands and knees, until another person releases them by placing their hands on the back of the person kneeling and side-vaulting over. As confidence grows make the vault a leapfrog. N.B. Some instruction on solid bases is essential.

Slither tag

When caught, lie stomach down until someone slithers over your back without using their hands. (This is very good for the midriff).

Bump tag

When caught, the child must hold on to a body part, e.g., nose, bottom, elbow, shoulder, hip. To release them, another child must make contact with the same body part which is sticking out. (This can be hilarious).

Memory and Sequencing Games

Colours

Each wall of the gym is given a different colour, i.e. red, yellow, blue, green. A central base is established to which the group must return after each run. A colour is called. All children run to that colour and back to base. The last two back are given a forfeit.

Next, use two colours at once, three colours, and finally four colours. Each time the sequence called must be followed. Variety can be added by hopping, skipping, walking, bouncing to the named colour.

N.B. As children become quicker and more mobile it is advisable to use markers at least a yard away from the gym walls, thus avoiding unnecessary collisions.

Captain's Calling

The same basic game as 'colours', with the base being called 'The Bridge' of the ship. The colours are replaced with bow, stern, port and starboard. Variety comes with the additional calls of:

Climb the rigging: the wallbars
Bombs away: falling flat to the ground
Captain's aboard: stop and salute
Scrub the deck: crawl on hands and knees
All clear: continue on your journey around the ship.

Tape Recorder Game — another memory game

Teacher calls instructions:	Children respond with:
Fast forward	Run forwards quickly
Play	Run forwards medium pace
Stop	Stop! Freeze!
Rewind	Run backwards
Eject	Star shape jump
Record	Spin on Tummy

Each new instruction should be introduced as the game progresses. Don't give them all at the beginning.

Memory and Sequencing Relays

Relays are by nature competitive and lively. It is always a popular move to give teams names and large numbers of points for results. However, as far as the children are concerned — and they are quite right — the fun which they have had during the competition is just as important as the result of the competition itself. Such relays provide excellent opportunities for teachers and assistants to mix the groups according to abilities and can be used to encourage the more able to help and assist their less able companions.

These relays can be the basis of the whole lesson, for example, by turning the lesson into your own school 'Olympics', or using a specific feature of the lesson to encourage memory and sequencing.

Example 1. Aim: to promote body awareness.

Team Mat   Cone
X X X X   △

1. Race to the cone and back
2. As above. Touch cone with nose
3. As above. Touch cone with left hand
4. As above. Touch cone with right hand
5. As above. Touch cone with nose/right hand, and left hand

Each time you add a body part or change the combination of body parts, give the team which is first 10 points and everyone else 8 points. This keeps the drama going longer.

Example 2. Aim: to improve range of mobility

Team Mat   Rounders Post
X X X X   ●

1. Run to the post and back
2. Hop to the post and back
3. Crawl to the post and back
4. Skip to the post and back
5. Bunny hop to the post and back
6. Run backwards to the post and back
7. Run to the post and hop back
8. Skip to the post and bunny hop back

Again, you can increase the combinations and vary them to maintain interest and enthusiasm.

Example 3. Aim: to use simple apparatus to add complexity of instruction

Team Mat	Bench	Hoop	Rounders Post
X X X X	├─────┤	○	●

Walk along the bench, go through the hoop and round the post.

The variations you can use are determined by the type of locomotion you introduce, e.g., crawl, run, hop through, in or around. You may also wish to introduce something to be carried, bounced, dribbled, balanced or rolled.

Rhythm and Rhyme Games

When you look at these you may be tempted to think that they are too infantile and should have been left behind in the nursery. Experience, however, has shown that if a gap in development exists, then you must get down to the lowest common denominator to make sure that everyone has a proper chance to start his/her progress on equal terms. Moreover, bear in mind that these rhythm and rhyme games will not only play an important part in your pupils' physical development, but will also provide the children with fun and entertainment as they develop. This is a point I have made before, and I make it again now, because I think it is important.

You may also like to bear in mind the possible very long-term consequences. If the children you teach enjoy the process of their own physical development, it is likely that they will be predisposed to take an active interest in the development of their own children when they become parents themselves; and the skills you have passed on will be passed on in turn from one generation to another. The psychological climate of the early years tends to fix the weather for the rest of life. Making it read *fair* at the start is so much more pleasant and so much more rewarding than *gloomy*.

Swimming

The priorities in primary school are:

to teach beginners to swim
to provide opportunities for swimmers to improve their personal
performance in the three main strokes

However, from the earliest stages, a variety of activities and
swimming stunts should be included in the programme because they
are fun to do and they help to develop skill and versatility in the
water.

Draw patterns on water with nose
Blow bubbles
Duck head and open eyes under water
Kneel on bottom of pool
Sit on bottom of pool
Blow a table tennis ball along surface of water
Pick up objects from bottom of pool
Push off and glide across pool — using float
                                             — with arms stretched in front
Glide on back
Back glide with sculling action — width, then length
Forward roll from standing
Backward roll from standing
Push off, from glide into forward roll
Push off, back glide into backward roll
Handstand
Surface dive
Swim through hoop
Swim through partner's legs
Swim width under water
Tandem swimming — one uses arms, one uses legs
Float for one minute
Starfish float, face downwards
Mushroom float

Shuttle relays

1. Walking
2. Swim — own choice of stroke
3. Swim — stroke stipulated
4. Swim with float, using float as baton

Practices for Beginners

(With the use of Arm bands and floats)

1. *Entry*
   a. Walk down the steps backwards, holding onto rails.
   b. Sitting on the side, place both hands to one side, turn onto tummy and lower body into water.
   c. Jumping into water.
2. Holding rail, walk across pool, sliding feet along the bottom.
3. Holding rail, kicking legs.
4. 'Washing' faces and hair with both hands.
5. Walking across pool bottom, blowing table tennis balls.
6. Push to side of the pool, arms extended.
7. Repeat, legs kicking.
8. 'Ring-a-Roses', submarines.
9. Attempt width front paddle.
10. Walking backwards.
11. Going to sleep — lie back. 'Wake up'!
12. Attempt one width on backs, legs kicking.
13. 'Farmer's in the den'
14. Swim through first hoop supine, 'rolley polley' swim through second hoop prone.
15. Floating: prone, supine, mushroom float.
16. Safe exit — steps or pool side.

Introduction of Ball Skills

In order to make progress in ball skills all children, and I do stress *all*, must feel confident that they can manipulate a ball on their own without assistance or having to share the experience with someone else. It is essential, then, that children work on their own with as many different types of ball as possible. They need to squeeze them, roll them, spin them, kick them and so forth, and observe how the ball moves and bounces (if at all) and so come to terms with its qualities of hardness, softness, texture and shape. All this is necessary tactile and observational experience which ought to precede, indeed must precede, the use of the ball in a team game of any kind.

Irrespective of which ball is used, an introduction to ball skills should take the following pattern:

1. Squeeze and collapse the ball with two hands
2. As above with one hand, then the other hand
3. Roll the ball with your hands and then chase it
4. As above with feet
5. Throw the ball with two hands at the ceiling
6. As above with one hand and then the other
7. Can we bounce the ball?
8. Can we head the ball?
9. Can we spin the ball?

Competition can be introduced when you think the individual is ready for it. This does not mean, however, that you need to start thinking in terms of 'sides', 'teams' or 'groups'. An individual player can compete with himself: the ball is the opponent. So each child can be challenged thus:

a. 'Who can squeeze the ball until it disappears?'
b. 'Who can throw it highest?'
c. 'Who can head it furthest?'
d. 'Who can catch it?'
e. 'Dribble the ball, who can stop it first'?

Children who previously will have had litttle opportunity in games to receive the ball, adore this lesson.

As someone who coaches soccer to a high level, I can honestly say that time spent on making sure that each individual is comfortable with a ball will pay big dividends when you begin to introduce the stages of having team mates, opposition and goals.

Those who are good at ball games always want to keep close to the ball, and this means that children who are not so confident feel cut out and nervous and inadequate. Engender in DMD children feelings of confidence and competence in relation to the ball itself, and you will find that they too begin to exhibit the traits previously associated only with the able bodied.

Athletics

All summer circuits are adapted from the IBM Ten Step Award Scheme, sponsored by IBM UK Ltd and organized by the Southern Counties AA. The children work in groups and repeat activities for a period of time. No scoring is involved, and activities should be repeated over 3 weeks.

Example 1

	A 10 Metre shuttle run	
D Seated soccer throw Collect ball and repeat	**Warm up area** (Stretching, Strengthening and tags)	**B** N W E S Compass run
	C Three standing jumps (repeat)	

Example 2

A
N
W   E
S
Compass run

D

**Warm up
activities**

B

Object pick-up
race (with items
placed along the
floor, from starting
line to finish)

15 m hop

C
Slalom run around
obstacles placed at
intervals in a line
along the floor

Example 3

A
Standing soccer
throw

D

**Warm up
activities**

B

N
W   E
S

50 m
skipping

C
Shuttle run

Index